Pretty Patchwork Quilts
Traditional Patterns with Appliqué Accents

Cyndi Walker

Martingale®
& COMPANY

Pretty Patchwork Quilts:
Traditional Patterns with Appliqué Accents
© 2012 by Cyndi Walker

That Patchwork Place® is an imprint of Martingale & Company®.

Martingale & Company
19021 120th Ave. NE, Ste. 102
Bothell, WA 98011-9511 USA
www.martingale-pub.com

Printed in China
17 16 15 14 13 12   8 7 6 5 4 3 2 1

Library of Congress Cataloging-in-Publication Data is available upon request.

ISBN: 978-1-60468-077-5

Mission Statement
Dedicated to providing quality products and service to inspire creativity.

CREDITS

President & CEO: Tom Wierzbicki
Editor in Chief: Mary V. Green
Design Director: Paula Schlosser
Managing Editor: Karen Costello Soltys
Technical Editor: Ellen Pahl
Copy Editor: Melissa Bryan
Production Manager: Regina Girard
Cover & Text Designer: Adrienne Smitke
Illustrator: Robin Strobel
Photographer: Brent Kane

Contents

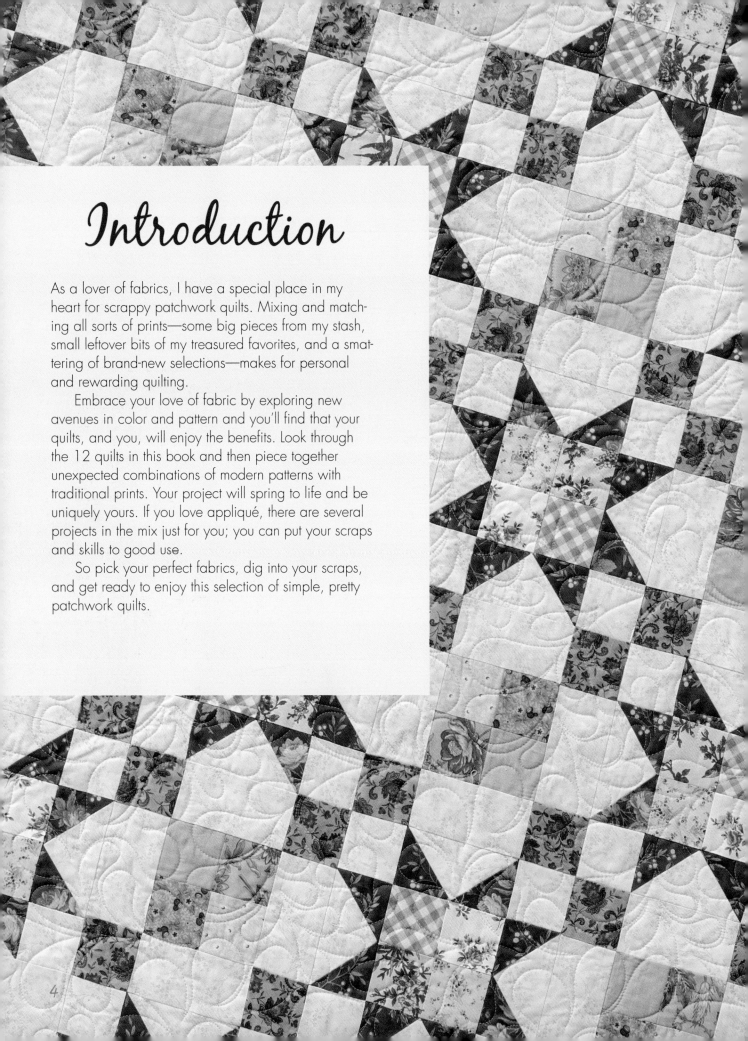

Introduction

As a lover of fabrics, I have a special place in my heart for scrappy patchwork quilts. Mixing and matching all sorts of prints—some big pieces from my stash, small leftover bits of my treasured favorites, and a smattering of brand-new selections—makes for personal and rewarding quilting.

Embrace your love of fabric by exploring new avenues in color and pattern and you'll find that your quilts, and you, will enjoy the benefits. Look through the 12 quilts in this book and then piece together unexpected combinations of modern patterns with traditional prints. Your project will spring to life and be uniquely yours. If you love appliqué, there are several projects in the mix just for you; you can put your scraps and skills to good use.

So pick your perfect fabrics, dig into your scraps, and get ready to enjoy this selection of simple, pretty patchwork quilts.

All of the projects featured in this book use high-quality, 100% cotton fabrics. Cotton is the go-to fabric of choice for quilters because of its versatility, vibrant colors, and crisp results when pressing. Choosing the best fabrics will ensure that your quilts are soft and comfy and will last through many years of use and enjoyment.

SELECTING YOUR FABRICS

In my eyes, this is one of the best parts of quilt-making—playing with fabric! The many beautiful options can be dizzying to choose from, as well as daunting to use. I'm not the first person to be gripped with fear and hesitation about cutting into (and potentially making a mess of) what appears to be the *perfect* set of fabrics.

But how do you achieve that perfect set of fabrics in the first place? First off, there's no such thing! There will always be some little piece that you'll go hunting for in the midst of making your quilt. Well, at least I do. . . . My process typically begins by rummaging through my stash and picking out a favorite fabric I've been longing to use. From there, I start pulling out prints that I think look lovely with it. I keep on pulling until I have a large assortment of fabrics. Surely, I think, this will make the most beautiful quilt. And sadly, this often isn't the case, but it's a great place to start. No more "blank paper" (or "blank design wall") syndrome to worry about. It's time to dive right in.

RAID YOUR STASH OR BUY MORE?

When it comes right down to it, I'd say that about half of my fabrics for each quilt come from my stash, and then I'm off shopping at the nearest (or not-so-nearest) quilt shop to "fill in the blanks," so to speak. Don't have a heap of stash fabric waiting to be used? No problem—your local quilt shop has more fabric than the eye can see, just waiting to be discovered. If you can't seem to find just the right piece of fabric, take another look at your fabrics and try switching out a few. Sometimes a keen editorial eye can take your fabric choices to the next level. There have been so many times when I've taken out the one piece of fabric I was dying to use, because it simply wasn't working. Your goal is to make the quilt just the way you want it, so avoid getting attached to something that isn't "playing nicely" with the other fabrics in the group.

Stash Bash

Want to build up your stash? Throw a little fabric swap party with your quilting friends. Invite each person to bring some prints to swap or donate, and then watch your fabric stash grow.

TO PREWASH OR NOT TO PREWASH?

Most quilters have an opinion—and are more than ready to share it—about whether to prewash fabrics before using them in a quilt, and all will stand their ground firmly on the subject. If you're still uncertain, knowing the pros and cons of each option can help you make this decision for yourself.

Prewashing your fabric removes any sizing and residual dyes, and allows the fabric to shrink before you sew it into your quilt. Quilts that will see heavy use and repeated laundering are good candidates for prewashed fabric, even if you typically don't take this preparatory step. Dark fabrics tend to bleed when washed, so it's best if that happens before you incorporate those fabrics into your quilt. Otherwise, you run the risk of a dark print bleeding onto a lovely adjacent cream fabric.

On the other hand, many quilts are made for artistic purposes rather than daily use. For the makers of these quilts, prewashing is less of an issue as the quilts will most likely never be washed, or are so heavily embellished that washing them isn't even an option. There are also those on the "I don't prewash" side who want the fabrics to shrink slightly when washed to give the finished quilt a puckered, antique look.

Prewash for Fusing

If you plan to use the fusible-appliqué method, be sure to prewash your fabrics. Chemicals used in the textile-manufacturing process can cause appliqué pieces to fuse poorly. Do not use any fabric softeners.

WORKING WITH PRINTS

Big florals, small dots, fancy stripes, and bold geometric prints are all among the pieces that play a role in my quilts. Variations in size, scale, and color are what make our quilt projects sing. With so many choices available, sometimes working with prints can be overwhelming, especially if you're feeling adventurous and want to try something new.

The scale of the print on the fabric plays a big part in the finished look of your quilt. Your choice of small "ditzy" prints, large dramatic prints, and everything in between gives you a wide range of opportunities to integrate scraps into your designs. Make the most of the fabric-selection process and embrace your basket of scraps.

Large-scale prints are a fun way to add variety to your quilt, and if cut and placed carefully, they can create the illusion of more than one fabric. Prints with motifs that seemed too large or difficult to use suddenly take on a new life. For example, a colorful, large-scale floral print can yield some very interesting results when cut up into small squares—each square will have its own personality and can be worked into your quilt to add variety and visual excitement.

Use What You Like

Have a favorite large-scale print, but one of the colors isn't quite right or there's really only one area of the print that you especially like? There are no rules in scrap quilting! Just cut out the area you like and use it.

Not to be forgotten, tiny prints add fun and texture to your quilt. Small-scale prints juxtaposed with large- and medium-scale prints can create interesting contrasts. For your next project, try auditioning a wide variety of prints before making your final decisions. If you're the proud owner of a beloved scrap pile, dive in and see what you already have on hand before heading off to your favorite quilt shop.

Tone-on-tone, or "tonal," fabrics can be a scrap quilter's best friend—well, heck, any quilter's best friend. These subtle prints add a sense of calm—a visual oasis—amid a sea of more active prints. When I shop for fabric, I often purchase tonal fabrics in my favorite colors or textures when I see them. These versatile fabrics have served me well when visual chaos threatened to overrun a work in progress. And last but not least, don't forget about your solids! Solid fabrics can add a much-needed dose of color and contrast to a busy quilt.

*Large-scale prints add variety
and interest to your quilts.*

*A medley of prints of different texture and
scale will create a richer scrap quilt.*

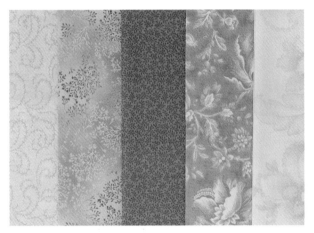

*Tonal fabrics with subtle print patterns provide
a visual resting place in a busy scrap quilt.*

*Why use just one fabric when you can use
several prints of the same color?*

BUILDING A SUCCESSFUL PALETTE

Many quilters struggle with color. Some actually dread choosing fabrics. To conquer a fear of color, begin by using colors you're comfortable with. Then slowly work your way up to more adventurous color combinations.

Broaden your horizons. If you've chosen the perfect yellow to use in your quilt, try substituting four different yellow prints in the same shade. Suddenly you've gone from using a single fabric to adding four new prints to your quilt. If you feel particularly brave, you can even try varying the value of these four new fabrics slightly—perhaps choosing one that is a shade lighter and one that is a shade darker. Be a fabric rebel! This approach can work with any color and is often the way I delve into my projects.

If you save scraps, this is the perfect time to dig deep into your stash. Since quilters frequently revisit favorite color schemes, it's very likely that leftovers from past projects will work in your current quilt. That 4" square of fabric you couldn't seem to part with can find a happy home where you least expect it.

If you don't have a scrap bag to draw from, check with your local quilt shop. The shop may sell scrap bags stuffed with odd cuts, remnants, and leftover pieces from the bolts on the shelves.

With each quilt you make, you'll accumulate scraps without even trying. Quilting can be a messy business, so recycle those leftovers!

COLOR INSPIRATION

As you begin a project, you may want to start with a piece of beautiful, inspirational fabric. The colors in a gorgeous floral print can be the inspiration for building an entire color palette, even if—ironically—that original inspiration piece is scrapped from your final fabric selection. If the color combinations of the inspiration fabric speak to you, the color palette is probably a good candidate for your next quilt.

Multicolored fabrics often find their way into my quilts as "blender fabrics." A blender fabric is one that allows me to create harmony between colors that might not otherwise go together. Imagine, for example, that you've fallen in love with a selection of pink and green fabrics at the quilt shop. The fabrics look OK together, but will they make a good quilt? If you have to ask yourself that question, the answer is usually, "not quite." Here is where the blenders work their magic. Find a beautiful fabric with both pink and green in the print, and see how it works with the various pink and green prints. Suddenly, one piece of fabric can make two other pieces of fabric play nicely together.

Blender fabrics create harmony between two or more diverse colors.

Briar Patch

Designed by Cyndi Walker; pieced by Debbie Gray; quilted by Pamela Dransfeldt

Nestled amongst the lattice and stars of this quilt are open areas just perfect for the making of a briar patch! Pick your best blue and orange prints to create this beautiful patchwork twist on some favorite patchwork blocks.

FINISHED QUILT: 56½" x 72½"
FINISHED BLOCKS: 8" x 8"

MATERIALS

Yardage is based on 42"-wide fabric.

4 yards of cream tonal fabric for block backgrounds and pieced border
1¾ yards *total* of assorted orange prints for Star blocks, Cross blocks, and pieced border
1⅛ yards *total* of assorted aqua prints for Star blocks, Cross blocks, and pieced border
⅓ yard of orange vine print for Star blocks
¼ yard of cream floral for Star blocks
⅝ yard of orange print for binding
4⅝ yards of fabric for backing
66" x 82" piece of batting

CUT THE FABRIC

From the assorted aqua prints, cut:
12 squares, 5¾" x 5¾"
105 squares, 2½" x 2½"

From the cream floral, cut:
8 squares, 4½" x 4½"

From the orange vine print, cut:
14 squares, 4½" x 4½"

From the assorted orange prints, cut:
12 squares, 5¾" x 5¾"
176 squares, 2½" x 2½"
204 squares, 1½" x 1½"

From the cream tonal fabric, cut:
4 strips, 5¾" x 42"; crosscut into 24 squares, 5¾" x 5¾"
27 strips, 2½" x 42"; crosscut *17* of the strips into:
    88 rectangles, 2½" x 4½"
    88 squares, 2½" x 2½"
24 strips, 1½" x 42"; crosscut into:
    68 rectangles, 1½" x 6½"
    68 rectangles, 1½" x 4½"
    68 rectangles, 1½" x 2½"

From the orange print for binding, cut:
7 strips, 2¼" x 42"

MAKE THE STAR BLOCKS

1. To make the center unit, lightly mark a diagonal line on the wrong side of four aqua 2½" squares. Align a marked square with one corner of a cream floral 4½" square as shown and sew along the line. Trim the excess fabric, leaving a ¼" seam allowance, and press the aqua triangle open. Repeat for the remaining three corners of the orange square to finish a center unit.

Make 1.

2. Lightly mark a diagonal line on the wrong side of two orange 2½" squares. Align a marked square with one end of a cream tonal 2½" x 4½" rectangle as shown and sew along the line. Trim the excess fabric, leaving a ¼" seam allowance, and press the seam allowance toward the orange triangle. Using the second marked orange square, repeat on the opposite end of the cream tonal rectangle to make a flying-geese unit. Make four.

Make 4.

3. Arrange the center unit, the flying-geese units, and four cream tonal 2½" squares as shown. Sew the pieces in each row together; press the seam allowances toward the triangles. Sew the rows together to complete a Star block; press as shown.

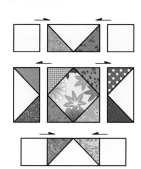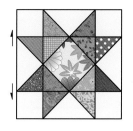

4. Repeat steps 1–3 to make 8 Star blocks using the cream floral 4½" squares. Make 14 Star blocks using the orange vine print 4½" squares.

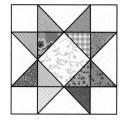

Make 8.   Make 14.

MAKE THE CROSS BLOCKS

1. Arrange one aqua 2½" square, four orange 1½" squares, and four cream tonal 1½" x 2½" rectangles as shown. Sew the pieces in each row together; press as shown. Sew the rows together to make the block center.

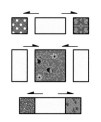

2. Arrange four orange 1½" squares, four cream tonal 1½" x 4½" rectangles, and the block center as shown. Sew the pieces in each row together; press toward the orange. Sew the rows together and press away from the center.

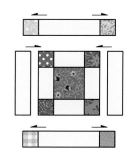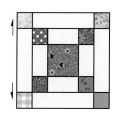

3. Arrange four orange 1½" squares and four cream tonal 1½" x 6½" rectangles as shown. Sew the pieces in each row together; press toward the orange. Sew the rows together and press away from the center. Repeat steps 1–3 to make 17 Cross blocks.

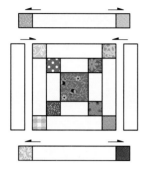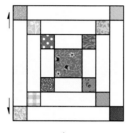

Make 17.

MAKE THE PIECED BORDERS

1. Lightly mark a diagonal line from corner to corner on the wrong side of the 24 cream tonal 5¾" squares.
2. With right sides together, align a marked cream square with an aqua 5¾" square. Stitch ¼" from the drawn line on each side. Cut along the drawn line to make two aqua half-square-triangle units; press toward the aqua.

3. Repeat step 2 with an orange 5¾" square and a marked cream square to make two orange half-square-triangle units.

4. Layer one aqua and one orange half-square-triangle unit together so that the cream half is facing the orange or aqua half of the other unit. Draw a diagonal line from corner to corner, perpendicular to the seam line. Sew ¼" from the drawn line on each side. Cut on the drawn line and press. Trim the Hourglass blocks to 4½" square.

5. Repeat steps 2–4 to make a total of 48 Hourglass blocks.
6. For the side borders, arrange 14 Hourglass blocks to make one long strip, placing every other unit so that the aqua and orange triangles are on opposite sides. Sew together and press the seam allowances in one direction. Make a second border strip that's a mirror image of the first.
7. Sew six cream tonal 2½" x 42" strips together to make one long strip. Cut into four strips, 2½" x 56½", and sew one strip to each long edge of both hourglass strips; press.

Make 1.

Make 1.

8. For the top and bottom borders, arrange 10 Hourglass blocks as you did before, placing every other unit so that the aqua and orange triangles are on opposite sides. Sew together and press in one direction. Sew a cream tonal 2½" x 40½" strip to each long edge of both hourglass strips; press toward the cream. Make a second border strip that's a mirror image of the first.

9. Sew a Star block to each end of the top and bottom border strips.

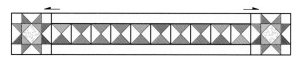

Make 1.

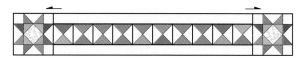

Make 1.

ASSEMBLE THE QUILT

1. Referring to the quilt assembly diagram below, arrange the Star blocks and Cross blocks in seven rows of five blocks each. Sew the blocks in each row together; press toward the Cross blocks. Sew the rows together; press in one direction.

2. Sew a long border strip to each side of the quilt center; press toward the border strip.

3. Sew the top and bottom border strips to the quilt center; press toward the border strip.

FINISH THE QUILT

For detailed instructions on the following steps, refer to "Finishing Techniques" on page 76.

1. Cut and piece the backing fabric with a vertical seam so that it measures 10" larger than both the length and width of the quilt top.

2. Layer the quilt top, batting, and backing together and baste.

3. Machine or hand quilt as desired.

4. Use the orange print 2¼"-wide strips to prepare the binding, and sew the binding to the quilt.

Sea Breeze

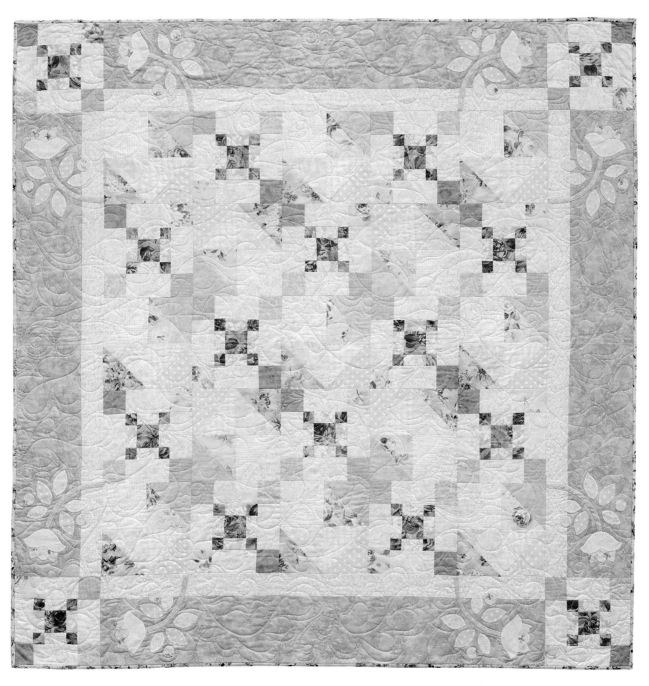

Designed, pieced, and quilted by Cyndi Walker

MATERIALS

Yardage is based on 42"-wide fabric.

⅞ yard of blue tonal fabric for outer border

⅔ yard of cream tonal fabric for Nine Patch blocks

⅜ yard *each* of 5 light-green prints for blocks and appliquéd leaves and flower tips

⅜ yard of cream print for inner border

⅓ yard of light-green tonal fabric for Nine Patch blocks

⅓ yard of green-and-red floral for Nine Patch blocks

¼ yard *each* of 6 light- to medium-blue prints for blocks

1 fat quarter of green fabric for appliquéd stems

⅛ yard of cream solid for appliquéd flower bodies

⅛ yard of light-yellow print for appliquéd flower centers and berries

½ yard of green print for binding

3⅔ yards of fabric for backing

66" x 66" piece of batting

⅜" bias bar

Clear monofilament or matching embroidery thread for machine appliqué

Water-soluble glue

CUT THE FABRIC

Patterns for the flowers, leaves, and berry are on page 19.

From *each* of blue prints 1–4, cut:

7 squares, 4⅞" x 4⅞"; cut each square in half diagonally to make 14 triangles (4 are extra)

From *each* of blue prints 5 and 6, cut:

16 squares, 2½" x 2½"

From *each* of light-green prints 1–4, cut:

7 squares, 4⅞" x 4⅞"; cut each square in half diagonally to make 14 triangles (4 are extra)

From light-green print 2, cut:

16 squares, 2½" x 2½"

Continued on page 16.

From light-green print 5, cut:
16 squares, 2½" x 2½"

From the *remainder* of the light-green prints, cut:
24 large leaves
16 small leaves
8 flower tips

From the green-and-red floral, cut:
1 strip, 2½" x 42"
4 strips, 1½" x 42"

From the light-green tonal fabric, cut:
2 strips, 2½" x 42"
2 strips, 1½" x 42"

From the cream tonal fabric, cut:
8 strips, 2½" x 42"; crosscut into 64 rectangles,
    2½" x 4½"

From the blue tonal fabric, cut:
4 strips, 6½" x 42"

From the cream print, cut:
4 strips, 2½" x 42"

From the green fat quarter, cut:
8 bias strips, 1⅛" x 10"

From the cream solid, cut:
8 flower bodies

From the light-yellow print, cut:
8 flower centers
16 berries

From the green print for binding, cut:
6 strips, 2¼" x 42"

MAKE THE BROKEN DISHES BLOCKS

1. Sew a blue triangle and a light-green triangle together along the diagonal edges to make a half-square-triangle unit; press toward the blue. Repeat to make a total of four half-square-triangle

units, using a different blue and green triangle for each unit.

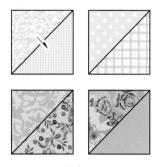

Make 4.

2. Arrange the four half-square-triangle units into two rows of two units each with the lighter green and blue triangles meeting in the center as shown. Sew the units in each row together and press in opposite directions for each row. Sew the rows together to complete the block. Repeat steps 1 and 2 to make a total of 13 Broken Dishes blocks.

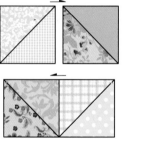
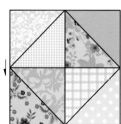

Make 13.

MAKE THE NINE PATCH BLOCKS

1. Sew a green-and-red floral 1½" x 42" strip to each long edge of a light-green tonal 2½" x 42" strip to make strip set A; press toward the floral. Make two strip sets. Cut the strip sets into a total of 32 segments, 1½" wide.

1½"

Strip set A.
Make 2. Cut 32 segments.

2. Sew a light-green tonal 1½" x 42" strip to each long edge of the green-and-red floral 2½" x 42" strip to make strip set B; press toward the floral. Cut the strip set into a total of 16 segments, 2½" wide.

2½"

Strip set B.
Make 1. Cut 16 segments.

3. Sew strip set A segments to opposite sides of a strip set B segment to complete a nine-patch center unit; press. Make a total of 16 center units.

Make 16.

4. Arrange two different blue 2½" squares, two different light-green 2½" squares, four cream tonal 2½" x 4½" rectangles, and one nine-patch center unit, placing the green and blue squares in opposite corners as shown. Sew the pieces in each row together; press away from the rectangles. Sew the rows together to complete a Nine Patch block; press. Repeat to make a total of 16 Nine Patch blocks. Four will be used for the border corners.

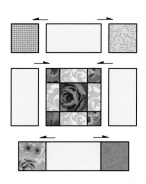 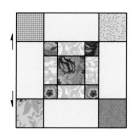

Make 16.

MAKE THE APPLIQUÉD BORDER

1. Sew a blue tonal 6½" x 42" strip and a cream print 2½" x 42" strip together along their long edges as shown; press toward the blue. Trim this unit to 40½" long to make a border strip. Repeat to make a total of four border strips.

2. Referring to "Bias Stems and Vines" on page 74 and following the manufacturer's instructions for the ⅜" bias bar, prepare the green 1⅛"-wide bias strips for appliqué. Make eight stems.

3. Referring to the placement diagram below, appliqué the pieces to each end of a border strip in the order listed, trimming the stem as necessary after positioning:

    1 stem
    1 flower tip
    1 flower center
    1 flower body
    3 large leaves
    2 small leaves
    2 berries

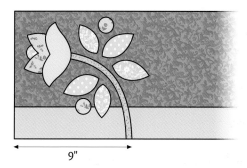

9"

4. Repeat step 3 to complete all four appliquéd border strips.

ASSEMBLE THE QUILT

1. Referring to the quilt assembly diagram below, arrange the Broken Dishes blocks and Nine Patch blocks into five rows of five blocks each, alternating them as shown. Sew the blocks into rows and press toward the Broken Dishes blocks. Sew the rows together to complete the quilt center; press in one direction.
2. Sew an appliquéd border strip to opposite sides of the quilt center; press toward the border.
3. Sew a Nine Patch block to each end of the remaining two appliquéd border strips; press toward the appliquéd border. Join these two border strips to the top and bottom of the quilt center; press toward the border.

FINISH THE QUILT

For detailed instructions on the following steps, refer to "Finishing Techniques" on page 76.

1. Cut and piece the backing fabric with a vertical or horizontal seam so that it measures 10" larger than both the length and width of the quilt top.
2. Layer the quilt top, batting, and backing together and baste.
3. Machine or hand quilt as desired.
4. Use the green print 2¼"-wide strips to prepare the binding, and sew the binding to the quilt.

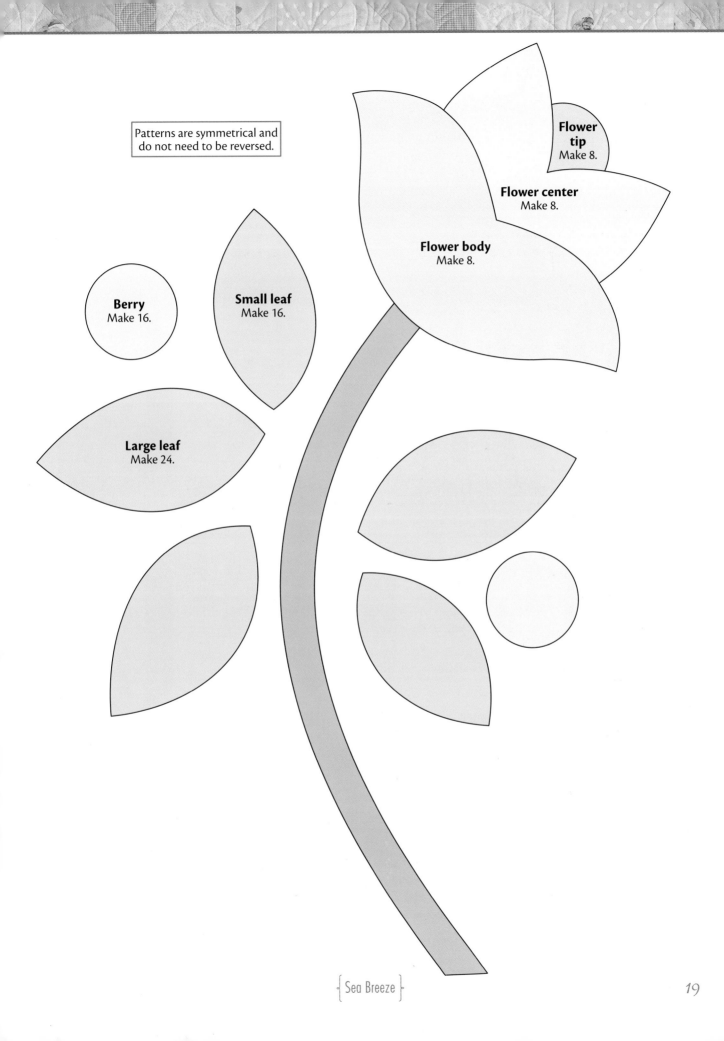

Patterns are symmetrical and do not need to be reversed.

Flower tip
Make 8.

Flower center
Make 8.

Flower body
Make 8.

Berry
Make 16.

Small leaf
Make 16.

Large leaf
Make 24.

Ginger Snap

Designed and pieced by Cyndi Walker; quilted by Pamela Dransfeldt

FINISHED QUILT: 44½" x 44½"
FINISHED BLOCKS: 16" x 16"

MATERIALS

Yardage is based on 42"-wide fabric.

1 yard of yellow tonal fabric for border and Nine Patch
border corner blocks
½ yard of green tonal fabric for appliquéd stems
½ yard *total* of assorted brown fabrics for blocks
½ yard *total* of assorted cream and tan fabrics for blocks
½ yard *total* of assorted green prints for appliquéd leaves
⅜ yard of small-scale cream floral for blocks
⅓ yard of cream tonal fabric for block centers
⅓ yard of green polka-dot fabric for appliquéd leaves
¼ yard of orange tonal fabric for appliquéd flowers and buds
⅛ yard of tan gingham fabric for blocks
3 fat eighths or scraps of assorted yellow prints for appliquéd
flowers
1 fat eighth of small-scale orange floral for appliquéd flowers
and bud centers
½ yard of orange print for binding
3 yards of fabric for backing
54" x 54" piece of batting
⅝" bias bar
Clear monofilament or matching embroidery thread for
machine appliqué
Water-soluble glue

CUT THE FABRIC

Patterns for the flowers and leaves are on page 25.

From the cream tonal fabric, cut:
4 squares, 8½" x 8½"

From the small-scale cream floral, cut:
4 strips, 2½" x 42"; crosscut into 16 rectangles, 2½" x 8½"

From the tan gingham fabric, cut:
1 strip, 2½" x 42"; crosscut into 16 squares, 2½" x 2½"

From the assorted cream and tan fabrics, cut:
4 sets of 8 matching squares, 2½" x 2½"
20 squares, 2½" x 2½"
64 squares, 1½" x 1½"

Continued on page 22.

From the assorted brown fabrics, cut:
16 rectangles, 2½" x 12½"

From the green tonal fabric, cut:
12 bias strips, 1⅝" x 14"

From the green polka-dot fabric, cut:
32 large leaves

From the orange tonal fabric, cut:
4 large flowers
12 flower buds

From the small-scale orange floral, cut:
4 medium flowers
16 bud centers

From the assorted yellow prints, cut:
12 matching bud centers
4 matching flower centers
4 sets of 4 matching flower buds

From the green polka-dot scraps and other assorted green prints, cut:
48 large leaves
32 small leaves

From the yellow tonal fabric, cut:
4 strips, 6½" x 32½"
1 strip, 2½" x 42"; crosscut into 16 squares, 2½" x 2½"

From the orange print, cut:
5 strips, 2¼" x 42"

MAKE THE BLOCKS

1. Arrange one cream 8½" square, four cream floral 2½" x 8½" rectangles, and four tan gingham 2½" squares as shown. Sew the pieces in each row together; press toward the rectangles. Sew the rows together to make a center unit; press away from the center square.

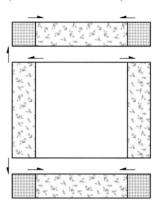

2. Lightly mark a diagonal line on the wrong side of two squares from each set of eight matching tan 2½" squares. Align a marked square with one end of a brown 2½" x 12½" rectangle and sew along the marked line. Trim the excess fabric, leaving a ¼" seam allowance, and press the seam allowances away from the brown rectangle. Repeat with a different square on the opposite end of the brown rectangle to make a side unit as shown. Make four units.

Make 4.

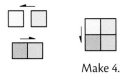

3. Arrange four assorted cream and tan 1½" squares as shown. Sew the pieces into rows and press in opposite directions. Sew the rows together to make a four-patch unit; press. Make four.

Make 4.

4. Arrange the center unit, side units, and four-patch units as shown. The corner fabrics in the triangles should match. Sew the units in each row together; press toward the side units. Sew the rows together to make a block; press in one direction. The block should measure 16½" x 16½".

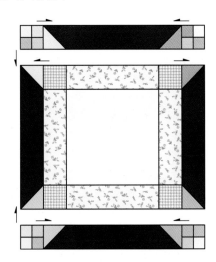

5. Repeat steps 1–4 to make a total of four blocks.

APPLIQUÉ THE BLOCKS AND BORDER

1. Referring to "Bias Stems and Vines" on page 74, prepare the bias stems using the green tonal 1⅝"-wide bias strips.
2. Cut four of the bias stems into four pieces, 3" long, for the flower stems.
3. Referring to the appliqué placement diagram above right, position four flower stems, one large flower, one medium flower, one flower center, four flower buds, four flower-bud centers, and eight large leaves onto a pieced block.

Block appliqué placement

4. Using clear monofilament or coordinating thread, stitch the appliqué pieces in place. Repeat for each of the remaining pieced blocks.
5. Referring to the border appliqué placement diagram, position two border stems, 12 large leaves, eight small leaves, three flower buds, and three flower-bud centers onto a yellow tonal 6½" x 32½" border strip. Using the clear monofilament or coordinating thread, stitch the appliqué pieces in place. Repeat for each of the remaining yellow border strips.

Border appliqué placement

MAKE THE BORDER CORNER BLOCKS

Arrange five cream 2½" squares and four yellow tonal 2½" squares into a block as shown. Sew the pieces in each row together; press toward the yellow. Sew the rows together to make a Nine Patch block for the border corner. Repeat to make a total of four blocks.

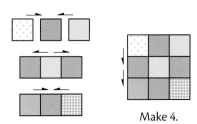

Make 4.

ASSEMBLE THE QUILT

1. Referring to the quilt assembly diagram below, arrange the appliqued blocks into two rows of two blocks each. Sew the blocks in each row together; press. Sew the rows together; press.
2. Sew an appliqued border panel to the opposite sides of the quilt center; press toward the border.
3. Sew a border corner block to each end of the remaining two appliqued border panels and press toward the border. Join these border strips to the top and bottom edges of the quilt center; press toward the border.

FINISH THE QUILT

For detailed instructions on the following steps, refer to "Finishing Techniques" on page 76.

1. Cut and piece the backing fabric with a vertical or horizontal seam so that it measures 10" larger than both the length and width of the quilt top.
2. Layer the quilt top, batting, and backing together and baste.
3. Machine or hand quilt as desired.
4. Use the orange print 2¼"-wide strips to prepare the binding, and sew the binding to the quilt.

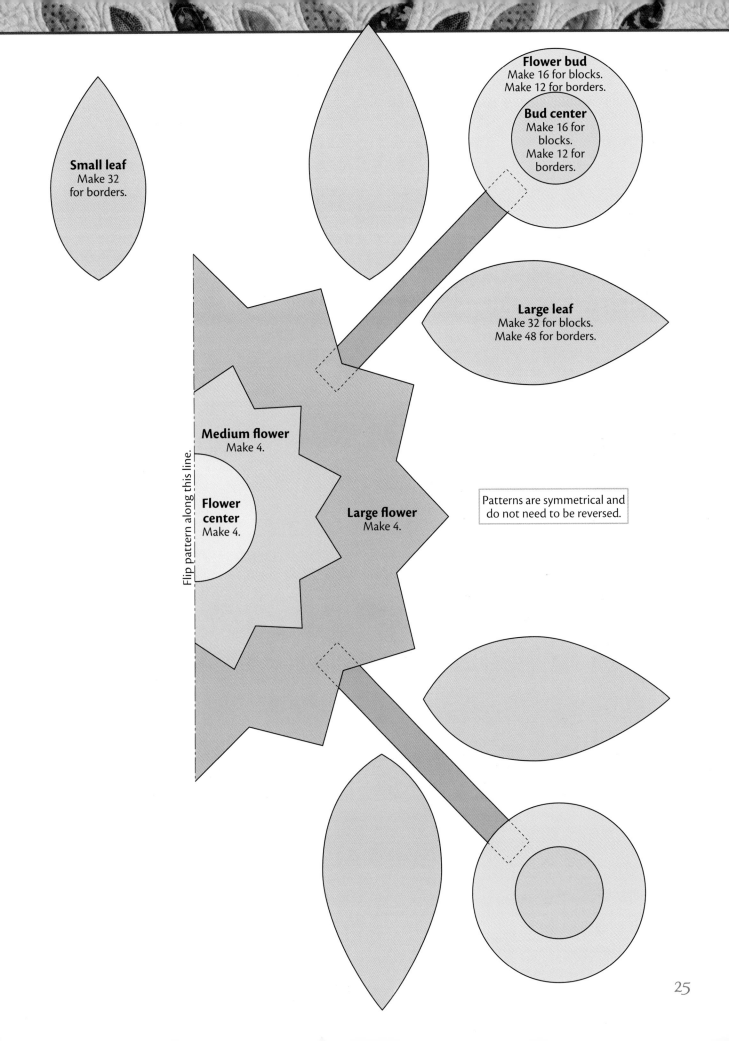

Small leaf
Make 32 for borders.

Flower bud
Make 16 for blocks.
Make 12 for borders.

Bud center
Make 16 for blocks.
Make 12 for borders.

Large leaf
Make 32 for blocks.
Make 48 for borders.

Flip pattern along this line.

Medium flower
Make 4.

Flower center
Make 4.

Large flower
Make 4.

Patterns are symmetrical and do not need to be reversed.

Granny Squares

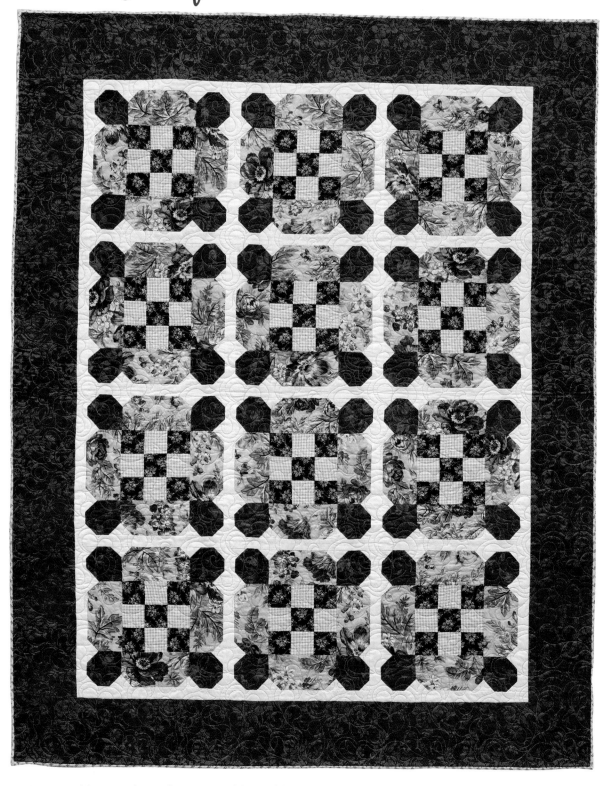

Designed by Cyndi Walker; pieced by Debbie Gray and Cyndi Walker; quilted by Pam Parker

This special quilt was inspired by those good old-fashioned crocheted granny squares—taken one step further. Large florals, beautiful reds, and some gingham for good measure make for a lovely end result.

FINISHED QUILT: 52½" x 65½"
FINISHED BLOCKS: 12" x 12"

MATERIALS

Yardage is based on 42"-wide fabric.

1⅔ yards of red tonal fabric for border
1 yard of cream solid for blocks and sashing
1 yard of tan floral for blocks
⅝ yard of red print for blocks
⅓ yard of brown print for nine-patch units
⅓ yard of green gingham for nine-patch units
⅝ yard of red-and-cream print for binding
3½ yards of fabric for backing
62" x 75" piece of batting

CUT THE FABRIC

From the green gingham, cut:
3 strips, 2½" x 42"; crosscut into 48 squares, 2½" x 2½"

From the brown print, cut:
4 strips, 2½" x 42"; crosscut into 60 squares, 2½" x 2½"

From the cream solid, cut:
21 strips, 1½ x 42"; crosscut 18 of the strips into:
    2 strips, 1½" x 40½"
    3 strips, 1½" x 38½"
    8 rectangles, 1½" x 12½"
    240 squares, 1½" x 1½"

From the tan floral, cut:
8 strips, 3½" x 42"; crosscut into 48 rectangles, 3½" x 6½"

From the red print, cut:
5 strips, 3½" x 42"; crosscut into 48 squares, 3½" x 3½"

From the red tonal fabric, cut on the *lengthwise* grain:
2 strips, 6½" x 53½"
2 strips, 6½" x 52½"

From the red-and-cream print, cut:
7 strips, 2¼" x 42"

MAKE THE BLOCKS

1. Arrange four green gingham 2½" squares and five brown 2½" squares as shown. Sew the squares in each row together; press toward the brown. Sew the rows together to make a nine-patch unit; press.

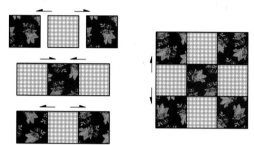

2. Lightly mark a diagonal line on the wrong side of two cream 1½" squares. Align a marked square with one corner of a tan floral 3½" x 6½" rectangle as shown and sew along the line. Trim the excess fabric, leaving a ¼" seam allowance, and press toward the cream triangle. Repeat on a second corner as shown to make a side unit. Make four side units.

Make 4.

3. Lightly mark a diagonal line on the wrong side of three cream 1½" squares. Align a marked square with one corner of a red 3½" square as shown and sew along the line. Trim the excess fabric, leaving a ¼" seam allowance, and press. Repeat for two more corners of the square to make a corner unit. Make four corner units.

Make 4.

4. Arrange the nine-patch unit, side units, and corner units as shown. Sew the units into rows; press toward the side units. Sew the rows together to complete a block; press.

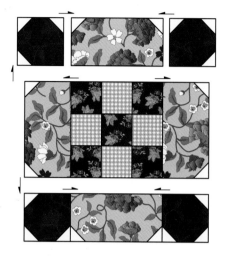

5. Repeat steps 1–4 to make a total of 12 blocks.

ADD THE SASHING AND BORDER

1. Referring to the quilt assembly diagram on the opposite page, arrange the blocks and sashing pieces into four rows of three blocks and two cream 1½" x 12½" rectangles each. Sew the blocks and sashing pieces into rows; press toward the sashing. Sew the rows together with a cream 1½" x 38½" strip between each row to finish the quilt center. Press toward the sashing.

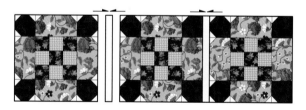

2. Piece the three cream 1½" x 42" strips together and cut two strips, 1½" x 51½". Sew the strips to the left and right edges of the quilt center; press away from the quilt center. Sew the cream 1½" x 40½" strips to the top and bottom edges of the quilt center; press away from the quilt center.

3. Sew the red 6½" x 53½" border strips to the left and right edges of the quilt center; press toward the border. Sew the red 6½" x 52½" border strips to the top and bottom edges of the quilt to finish the quilt top; press toward the border.

FINISH THE QUILT

For detailed instructions on the following steps, refer to "Finishing Techniques" on page 76.

1. Cut and piece the backing fabric with a horizontal seam so that it measures 10" larger than both the length and width of the quilt top.
2. Layer the quilt top, batting, and backing together and baste.
3. Machine or hand quilt as desired.
4. Use the red-and-cream print 2¼"-wide strips to prepare the binding, and sew the binding to the quilt.

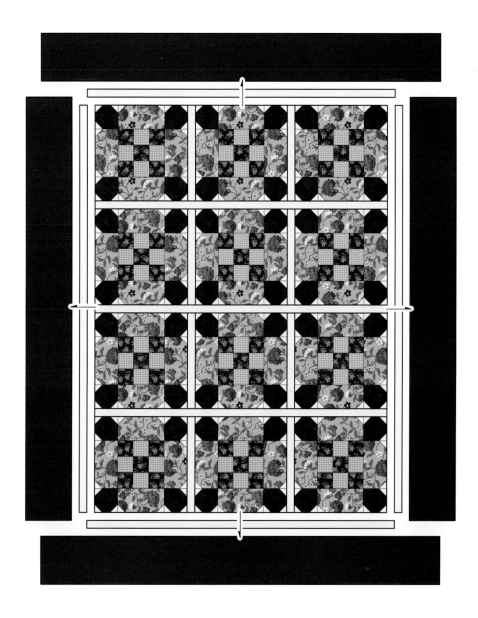

Tilted Spools

Designed by Cyndi Walker; pieced by Debbie Gray; quilted by Pamela Dransfeldt

The Spool block is a traditional favorite and I have to say, it's now a favorite of mine too! Dive into your stash and see what you come up with for this scrappy—and easy—spin on the Spool block.

FINISHED QUILT: 48½" x 64½"
FINISHED BLOCKS: 8" x 8"

MATERIALS

Yardage is based on 42"-wide fabric.

2⅝ yards *total* of assorted cream prints for blocks
1⅜ yards *total* of assorted aqua, tan, pink, and green prints for blocks
½ yard of golden yellow print for binding
3¼ yards of fabric for backing
58" x 74" piece of batting

CUT THE FABRIC

From the assorted cream prints, cut:
48 squares, 5" x 5"
48 pairs of squares, 4½" x 4½", to match the 5" squares (96 total)

From the assorted aqua, tan, pink, and green prints, cut:
48 squares, 5" x 5"
48 pairs of matching squares, 2½" x 2½" (96 total)

From the golden yellow print, cut:
6 strips, 2¼" x 42"

MAKE THE BLOCKS

1. Choose one cream 5" square and two cream 4½" squares, all from the same print. Choose one assorted-color 5" square and two matching colored 2½" squares that coordinate with the chosen 5" square.
2. Lightly mark a diagonal line on the wrong side of the cream 5" square. With right sides together, layer the assorted-color 5" square and the marked cream square; sew ¼" from the drawn line on each side. Cut along the drawn line to make two half-square-triangle units; press toward the colored print. Trim the unit to 4½" x 4½".

3. Lightly mark a diagonal line on the wrong side of the two assorted-color 2½" squares. Align a marked square with one corner of a cream 4½" square and sew along the marked line. Trim the excess fabric, leaving a ¼" seam allowance, and press the seam allowance toward the corner. Repeat to make two corner units.

Make 2.

4. Arrange the two half-square-triangle units and the two corner units as shown. Sew the units in each row together; press toward the half-square-triangle units. Sew the rows together to complete the block; press.

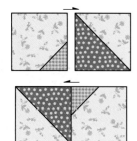

5. Repeat steps 1–4 to make a total of 48 blocks.

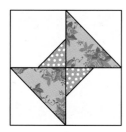

Make 48.

ASSEMBLE THE QUILT

Referring to the quilt assembly diagram below, arrange the blocks into eight rows of six blocks each, alternating the angle of the spools from block to block. Sew the blocks in each row together, pressing the seams in opposite directions from row to row. Sew the rows together and press all seam allowances in one direction to complete the quilt top.

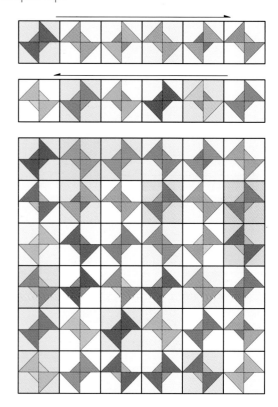

FINISH THE QUILT

For detailed instructions on the following steps, refer to "Finishing Techniques" on page 76.

1. Cut and piece the backing fabric with a horizontal seam so that it measures 10" larger than both the length and width of the quilt top.
2. Layer the quilt top, batting, and backing together and baste.
3. Machine or hand quilt as desired.
4. Use the golden yellow 2¼"-wide strips to prepare the binding, and sew the binding to the quilt.

Honey Bee

Designed and pieced by Cyndi Walker; quilted by Pamela Dransfeldt

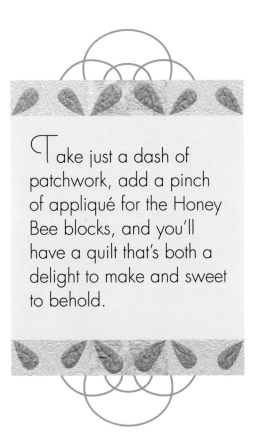

Take just a dash of patchwork, add a pinch of appliqué for the Honey Bee blocks, and you'll have a quilt that's both a delight to make and sweet to behold.

MATERIALS

Yardage is based on 42"-wide fabric.

1⅓ yards *total* of assorted blue, peach, green, and yellow prints for blocks and pieced outer border
⅝ yard of cream tonal fabric for blocks
⅜ yard of peach solid for inner border
⅜ yard of peach tonal fabric for appliquéd teardrops
⅓ yard of yellow tonal fabric for blocks
⅜ yard of peach floral for binding
3 yards of fabric for backing
54" x 54" piece of batting
Clear monofilament or matching embroidery thread for machine appliqué
Water-soluble glue

CUT THE FABRIC

Patterns for the teardrops are on page 37.

From the assorted blue, peach, green, and yellow prints, cut *a total of*:
16 strips, 2½" x 42"

From the cream tonal fabric, cut:
4 strips, 4½" x 42"; crosscut into 16 rectangles, 4½" x 8½"

From the yellow tonal fabric, cut:
2 strips, 4½" x 42"; crosscut into 16 squares, 4½" x 4½"

From the peach tonal fabric, cut:
16 large teardrops
32 small teardrops

From the peach solid, cut:
2 strips, 2½" x 36½"
2 strips, 2½" x 32½"

From the peach floral, cut:
5 strips, 2¼" x 42"

MAKE THE BLOCKS

1. Selecting different colors, sew together four assorted blue, peach, green, and yellow 2½" x 42" strips along the long edges to make a strip set. Repeat this process for the remaining assorted strips to make a total of four strip sets. Cut each strip set into 14 segments, 2½" wide, for a total of 56 segments.

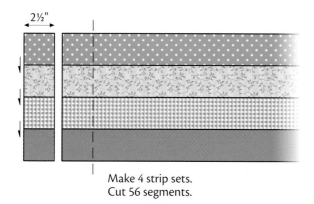

Make 4 strip sets.
Cut 56 segments.

2. Arrange four different strip-set segments into rows and sew together; press in either direction. Make four units. The remaining strip-set segments will be used later in the pieced border.

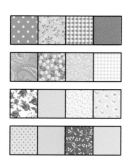
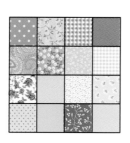

Make 4.

3. Arrange the block center, four cream tonal 4½" x 8½" rectangles, and four yellow tonal 4½" squares as shown. Sew the pieces into rows; press as shown. Sew the rows together to form the pieced block; press away from the block center. Make four blocks.

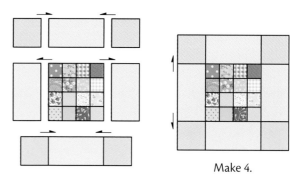

Make 4.

APPLIQUÉ THE BLOCKS

1. Referring to the appliqué placement diagram below, position four large teardrops and eight small teardrops onto a pieced block.
2. Using clear monofilament or coordinating thread, stitch the appliqué pieces in place.

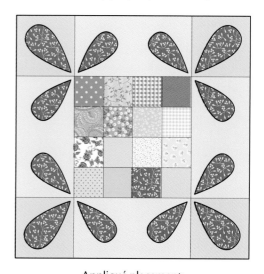

Appliqué placement

3. Repeat the appliqué process for each of the remaining three blocks.

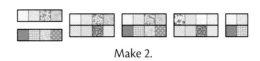

ASSEMBLE THE QUILT AND ADD THE BORDERS

1. Referring to the quilt assembly diagram below, arrange four appliqued blocks into two rows of two blocks each. Sew the blocks together in rows; press in opposite directions. Sew the rows together to make the quilt center.
2. Sew the peach solid 2½" x 32½" strips to the left and right edges of the quilt center; press toward the border. Sew the peach solid 2½" x 36½" strips to the top and bottom edges of the quilt center; press toward the border.
3. Using the leftover strip-set segments, sew 32 segments together in pairs to make 16 units for the border strips. Separate eight segments into two units each and make eight four-patch units. Sew the pairs and four-patch units into rows as shown; make two of each.
4. Sew the shorter pieced border strips to the left and right edges of the quilt; press toward the pieced border. Sew the remaining pieced

border strips to the top and bottom edges of the quilt; press toward the pieced border.

Make 2.

Make 2.

FINISH THE QUILT

For detailed instructions on the following steps, refer to "Finishing Techniques" on page 76.

1. Cut and piece the backing fabric with a vertical seam so that it measures 10" larger than both the length and width of the quilt top.
2. Layer the quilt top, batting, and backing together and baste.
3. Machine or hand quilt as desired.
4. Use the peach floral 2¼"-wide strips to prepare the binding, and sew the binding to the quilt.

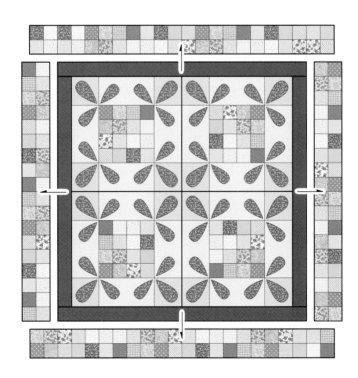

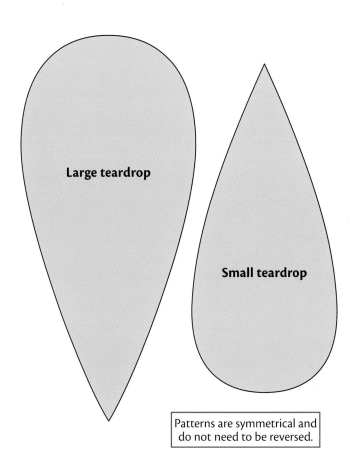

Large teardrop

Small teardrop

Patterns are symmetrical and
do not need to be reversed.

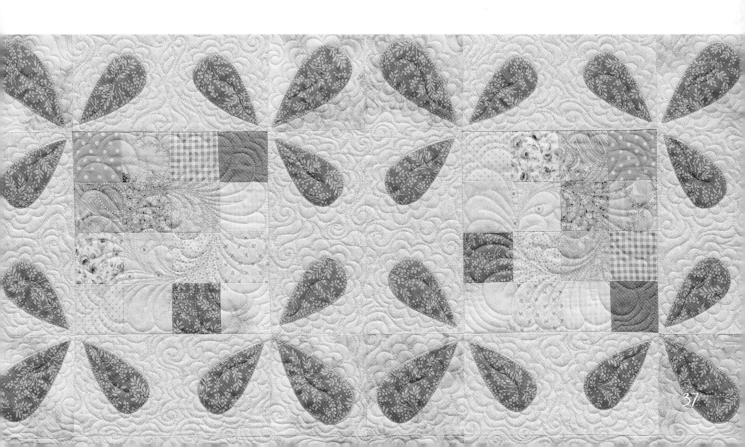

Shooting Stars

Designed and pieced by Cyndi Walker; quilted by Pamela Dransfeldt

The bright lights and cascading fireworks of the Fourth of July inspired this quilt of simple stars and Nine Patch blocks. Pick your favorite reds, blues, and creams and you'll be well on your way to creating this star-studded attraction.

FINISHED QUILT: 45¾" x 57"
FINISHED BLOCKS: 8" x 8"

MATERIALS

Yardage is based on 42"-wide fabric.

2⅜ yards of cream tonal fabric for blocks and setting triangles
⅞ yard of red floral for Star blocks
⅓ yard of aqua floral for Nine Patch blocks
1 fat quarter *each* of 5 assorted tan prints for Star blocks
1 fat quarter *each* of 3 assorted aqua prints for Nine Patch blocks
½ yard of aqua print for binding
3⅛ yards of fabric for backing
55" x 67" piece of batting

CUT THE FABRIC

From *each* of the 5 assorted tan fat quarters, cut:
2 strips, 2½" x 21"

From *each* of the 3 assorted aqua fat quarters, cut:
2 strips, 2½" x 21"

From the red floral, cut:
10 strips, 2½" x 42"; crosscut into 160 squares, 2½" x 2½"

From the cream tonal fabric, cut:
4 squares, 12⅝" x 12⅝"; cut each square into quarters diagonally to make 16 side setting triangles (2 are extra)
2 squares, 6⅝" x 6⅝"; cut each square in half diagonally to make 4 corner setting triangles
21 strips, 2½" x 42"; crosscut into:
    128 rectangles, 2½" x 4½"
    80 squares, 2½" x 2½"

From the aqua floral, cut:
3 strips, 2½" x 42"; crosscut into 48 squares, 2½" x 2½"

From the aqua print for binding, cut:
6 strips, 2¼" x 42"

MAKE THE FOUR-PATCH UNITS

1. Sew together two assorted tan 2½" x 21" strips along their long edges to make a strip set; press. Make five strip sets. Cut each strip set into eight segments, 2½" wide, to make a total of 40 tan strip-set segments.

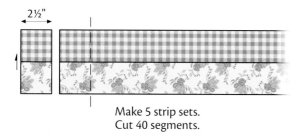

Make 5 strip sets.
Cut 40 segments.

2. Arrange two segments as shown and sew together to make a four-patch unit; press. Make 20 tan four-patch units.

Make 20.

3. Repeat steps 1 and 2 using the assorted aqua strips. Make three strip sets and cut 24 segments to make 12 aqua four-patch units.

Make 12.

MAKE THE STAR BLOCKS

1. Draw a diagonal line on the wrong side of each red floral 2½" square.
2. Align a marked square with one end of a cream tonal 2½" x 4½" rectangle as shown and sew along the line. Trim the excess fabric, leaving a ¼" seam allowance, and press the red triangle open. Repeat on the opposite end

of the rectangle to make a flying-geese unit. Make four flying-geese units.

Make 4.

3. Arrange the four flying-geese units, four cream 2½" squares, and one tan four-patch unit as shown. Sew the pieces in each row together; press. Sew the rows together to finish the Star block; press. Repeat steps 2 and 3 to make a total of 20 Star blocks.

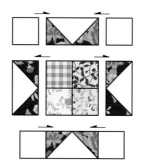
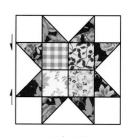

Make 20.

MAKE THE NINE PATCH BLOCKS

Arrange four cream tonal 2½" x 4½" rectangles, four aqua floral 2½" squares, and one aqua four-patch unit as shown. Sew the pieces in each row together; press toward the aqua. Sew the rows together to complete a Nine Patch block; press. Make 12 blocks.

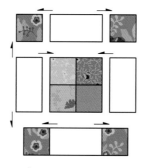
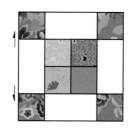

Make 12.

ASSEMBLE THE QUILT

1. Referring to the quilt assembly diagram below, arrange the Star blocks, Nine Patch blocks, side setting triangles, and corner setting triangles into diagonal rows.
2. Sew the blocks and triangles in each row together; press toward the Nine Patch blocks and triangles. Sew the rows together to complete the quilt top. Press the seam allowances in one direction.

FINISH THE QUILT

For detailed instructions on the following steps, refer to "Finishing Techniques" on page 76.
1. Cut and piece the backing fabric with a horizontal seam so that it measures 10" larger than both the length and width of the quilt top.
2. Layer the quilt top, batting, and backing together and baste.
3. Machine or hand quilt as desired.
4. Use the aqua print 2¼"-wide strips to prepare the binding, and sew the binding to the quilt.

Robin's Roost

Designed, pieced, and appliquéd by Cyndi Walker; quilted by Pamela Dransfeldt

I love red, and what better way to show off this bold, beautiful hue than in a scrap quilt? A fun zigzag border links the graceful appliqué along the outside of the quilt with the red-and-green patchwork stars in the center. It's a perfect combination to show off colors, piecing, and appliqué.

MATERIALS

Yardage is based on 42"-wide fabric.

1⅛ yards of cream tonal fabric for blocks and pieced border

1⅛ yards of red tonal fabric for pieced border and outer border

1 yard *total* of assorted red prints for blocks and appliquéd flower centers

½ yard *total* of assorted cream prints for blocks and appliquéd middle flowers and berries

½ yard of green tonal fabric for appliquéd vines

¼ yard *each* of 3 assorted green prints for blocks

¼ yard *total* of assorted green prints for appliquéd leaves

¼ yard of cream floral print for appliquéd outer flowers

½ yard of cream floral striped fabric for binding

3¼ yards of fabric for backing

58" x 58" piece of batting

½" bias bar

Clear monofilament or matching embroidery thread for machine appliqué

Water-soluble glue

CUT THE FABRIC

Patterns for the flowers, leaf, and berry are on page 47.

From *each* of the 3 green prints for blocks, cut:

4 squares, 5¼" x 5¼"; cut each square into quarters diagonally to make 16 triangles (48 total)

From the assorted red prints, cut:

176 squares, 2½" x 2½"

8 matching flower centers

From the cream tonal fabric, cut:

4 squares, 5¼" x 5¼"; cut each square into quarters diagonally to make 16 triangles

11 strips, 2½" x 42"; crosscut into:
    88 rectangles, 2½" x 4½"
    4 squares, 2½" x 2½"

From the red tonal fabric for borders, cut:

4 strips, 6½" x 36½"

4 strips, 2½" x 42"; crosscut into 64 squares, 2½" x 2½"

Continued on page 44.

From the cream floral print, cut:
8 outer flowers

From the assorted cream prints, cut:
20 squares, 2½" x 2½"
8 matching middle flowers
16 matching berries

From the assorted green prints for appliqué, cut:
48 leaves

From the green tonal fabric for vines, cut:
8 bias strips, 1⅜" x 22"

From the cream floral striped fabric, cut:
6 strips, 2¼" x 42"

MAKE THE UNITS

1. Arrange four assorted red print 2½" squares together to make a four-patch unit. Sew the squares into rows and press. Sew the rows together; press. Make 24 four-patch units.

Make 24.

2. Lightly mark a diagonal line on the wrong side of the remaining 80 assorted red print 2½" squares.

3. Align a marked square with one end of a 2½" x 4½" cream fabric rectangle as shown and sew along the line. Trim the excess fabric, leaving a ¼" seam allowance, and press toward the red triangle. Repeat this process with a second red square on the opposite end of the cream rectangle to make a flying-geese unit. Make a total of 40 flying-geese units.

Make 40.

4. Arrange one four-patch unit, two flying-geese units, and one 2½" assorted cream square as shown. Sew the units in each row together; press toward the flying-geese units. Sew the rows together to make a corner unit; press toward the four-patch unit. Make 20 corner units.

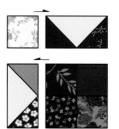

Make 20.

5. Arrange one cream triangle and one triangle from each of the three greens as shown. Sew the triangles together in pairs; press in opposite directions. Sew the pairs of triangles together to make an hourglass unit; press. Make 16 hourglass units.

Make 16.

6. Sew a 2½" x 4½" cream fabric 1 rectangle to the cream triangle of an hourglass unit to make a side unit; press toward the rectangle. Make 16 side units.

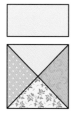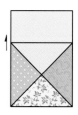

Make 16.

7. Repeat steps 2 and 3 to mark the 64 red tonal 2½" squares and sew to the 32 remaining 2½" x 4½" rectangles of cream fabric. Make 32 flying-geese units for the pieced borders.

ASSEMBLE THE BLOCKS
AND QUILT CENTER

1. Arrange four corner units, four side units, and one four-patch unit as shown. Sew the units into rows; press. Sew the rows together to complete a block; press away from the center. Make four blocks.

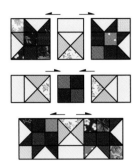 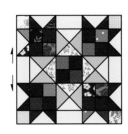

Make 4.

2. Sew the blocks together into two rows of two blocks each; press each row in the opposite direction. Sew the rows together to complete the quilt center.

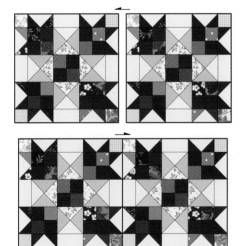

ADD THE INNER BORDER

1. Sew together eight flying-geese units to make an inner-border strip; press seam allowances in one direction. Make four inner-border strips.

Make 4.

2. Sew an inner-border strip to both the left and right edges of the quilt center; press toward the border. Sew a 2½" cream square to each end of the remaining two inner-border strips; press away from the cream squares. Sew these strips to the top and bottom edges of the quilt center; press toward the border. Refer to the diagram on page 46.

APPLIQUÉ AND ADD
THE OUTER BORDER

1. Referring to "Bias Stems and Vines" on page 74, prepare ½" bias vines using the green tonal 1⅜"-wide bias strips.

2. Referring to the placement diagram below and the quilt photograph on page 42, position two vines, two cream floral print large flowers, two cream middle flowers, two red flower centers, 12 leaves, and four berries on a red 6½" x 36½" strip. Trim the vines if needed. Using the clear monofilament or coordinating thread, stitch the appliqué pieces in place to make an appliqued border strip. Refer to "Machine Appliqué" on page 74 for details as needed. Make four appliquéd borders.

Make 4.

3. Sew an appliquéd border strip to both the left and right edges of the quilt center; press toward the appliquéd border. Sew a corner unit to each end of the remaining two appliquéd border strips. Sew these two strips to the top and bottom edges of the quilt center; press toward the appliquéd border.

FINISH THE QUILT

For detailed instructions on the following steps, refer to "Finishing Techniques" on page 76.

1. Cut and piece the backing fabric with a horizontal or vertical seam so that it measures 10" larger than both the length and width of the quilt top.
2. Layer the quilt top, batting, and backing together and baste.
3. Machine or hand quilt as desired.
4. Use the floral striped 2¼"-wide strips to prepare the binding, and sew the binding to the quilt.

{ Robin's Roost }

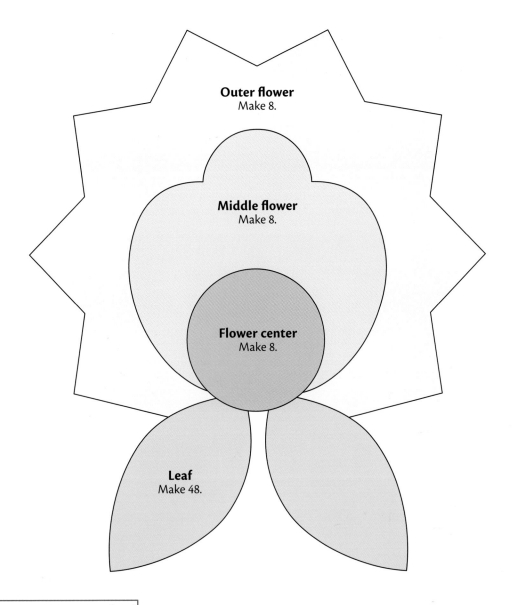

Outer flower
Make 8.

Middle flower
Make 8.

Flower center
Make 8.

Leaf
Make 48.

Patterns are symmetrical and
do not need to be reversed.

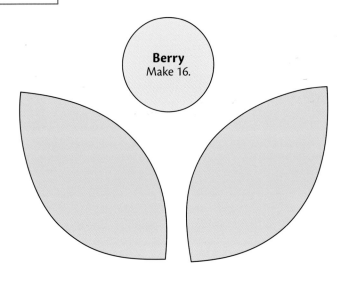

Berry
Make 16.

Skip to My Lou

Designed and pieced by Cyndi Walker; quilted by Pamela Dransfeldt

If you love pink or have someone in your life who does, grab your pink scraps and go for it! Or, pick your own favorite colors and have a great time pairing them up for this scrappy, sweet, and simple little Pinwheel quilt. It will go together in a jiffy.

FINISHED QUILT: 52½" x 68½"
FINISHED BLOCKS: 8" x 8"

MATERIALS

Yardage is based on 42"-wide fabric.

2¼ yards *total* of assorted pink and tan prints for Four Patch blocks and pieced border
1⅓ yards of cream tonal fabric for Pinwheel blocks and inner border
⅞ yard of pink tonal fabric for Pinwheel blocks
⅝ yard of tan print for binding
3½ yards of fabric for backing
62" x 78" piece of batting

CUT THE FABRIC

From the cream tonal fabric, cut:
5 strips, 5" x 42"; crosscut into 36 squares, 5" x 5"
6 strips, 2½" x 42"

From the pink tonal fabric, cut:
5 strips, 5" x 42"; crosscut into 36 squares, 5" x 5"

From the assorted pink and tan fabrics, cut:
124 squares, 4½" x 4½"

From the tan print, cut:
7 strips, 2¼" x 42"

MAKE THE PINWHEEL BLOCKS

1. Lightly mark a diagonal line on the wrong side of two cream tonal 5" squares. With right sides together, align a marked cream square and one pink tonal 5" square.
2. Stitch ¼" from the drawn line on each side. Cut along the drawn line to make two half-square-triangle units; press seam allowances toward the pink. Trim the units to 4½" square. Repeat to make a total of 72 half-square-triangle units.

Make 72.

3. Arrange four half-square-triangle units as shown. Sew the units in each row together; press the rows in opposite directions. Sew the rows together to make a Pinwheel block. Repeat to make a total of 18 Pinwheel blocks.

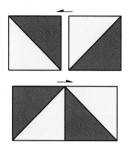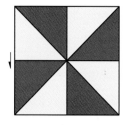

Make 18.

MAKE THE FOUR PATCH BLOCKS

Arrange four assorted pink and tan 4½" squares as shown. Sew the squares in each row together; press seam allowances in each row in the opposite direction. Sew the rows together to make a Four Patch block. Repeat to make a total of 17 Four Patch blocks.

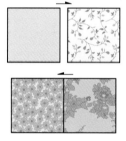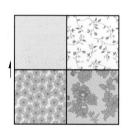

Make 17.

MAKE THE PIECED BORDER STRIPS

1. Arrange 15 assorted pink and tan 4½" squares as shown. Sew the squares together to make a long pieced border strip; press in one direction. Make two strips.

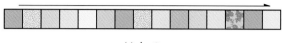

Make 2.

2. Repeat step 1 with 13 assorted pink and tan 4½" squares to make two short pieced border strips.

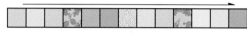

Make 2.

ASSEMBLE THE QUILT

1. Arrange the Pinwheel and Four Patch blocks into seven rows of five blocks each, alternating the blocks as shown. Sew the blocks in each row together; press toward the Four Patch blocks. Sew the rows together to make the quilt center. Press all seam allowances in one direction.

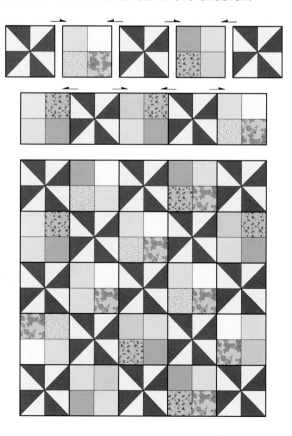

2. Sew the cream tonal 2½" x 42" strips together to make one long strip. Cut two strips, 2½" x 56½", and two strips, 2½" x 44½".

3. Sew the cream 2½" x 56½" strips to the left and right edges of the quilt center; press toward the border. Sew the cream 2½" x 44½" strips to the top and bottom edges of the quilt center; press toward the border.

4. Sew the long pieced border strips to the left and right edges of the quilt; press toward the pieced border. Sew the short pieced border strips to the top and bottom edges of the quilt to finish the quilt top; press toward the pieced border.

FINISH THE QUILT

For detailed instructions on the following steps, refer to "Finishing Techniques" on page 76.

1. Cut and piece the backing fabric with a horizontal seam so that it measures 10" larger than both the length and width of the quilt top.

2. Layer the quilt top, batting, and backing together and baste.

3. Machine or hand quilt as desired.

4. Use the tan print 2¼"-wide strips to prepare the binding, and sew the binding to the quilt.

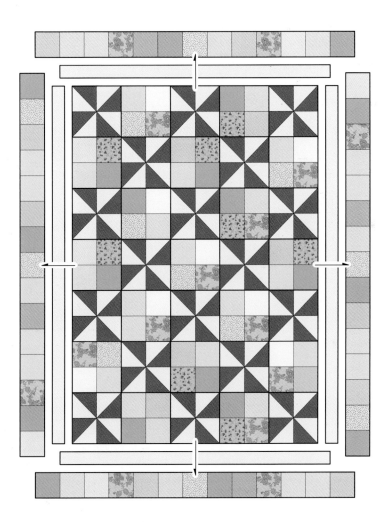

Sweet Charity

Designed and appliquéd by Cyndi Walker; pieced by Debbie Gray; quilted by Kate Sullivan

Τhis quilt comes to life with a radiant collection of fall colors. Scrappy Star blocks and a lovely appliquéd-vine border offer plenty of chances to dip into your scraps, boost your color confidence, and enjoy making a fabulous quilt.

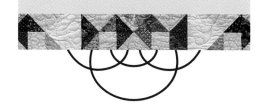

MATERIALS

Yardage is based on 42"-wide fabric.

1 ⅞ yards of cream tonal fabric for blocks, sashing, and borders
¾ yard *total* of assorted green prints for blocks and appliquéd leaves
¾ yard of tan print for blocks
⅔ yard *total* of assorted brown prints for blocks
½ yard *total* of assorted orange and red prints for blocks and sashing units
½ yard of green tonal fabric for appliquéd vines
⅓ yard of green floral for block centers
¼ yard of tan polka-dot fabric for blocks
¼ yard of tan gingham fabric for blocks
½ yard of orange print for binding
3¾ yards of fabric for backing
66" x 66" piece of batting
⅜" bias bar
Clear monofilament or matching embroidery thread for machine appliqué
Water-soluble glue

CUT THE FABRIC

The pattern for the leaf is on page 58.

From the assorted orange and red prints, cut:
112 squares, 2½" x 2½"
4 strips, 1½" x 42"*

From the green floral, cut:
9 squares, 4½" x 4½"

From the tan print, cut:
9 strips, 2½" x 42"; crosscut into:
    36 rectangles, 2½" x 4½"
    72 squares, 2½" x 2½"

From the tan polka-dot fabric, cut:
3 strips, 2½" x 42"; crosscut into 36 squares, 2½" x 2½"

*Cut each of these strips from a different orange or red fabric.

Continued on page 54.

From the tan gingham fabric, cut:
3 strips, 2½" x 42"; crosscut into 36 squares,
  2½" x 2½"

From the assorted green prints, cut:
72 squares, 2½" x 2½"
96 leaves

From the assorted brown prints, cut:
32 rectangles, 2½" x 4½"
60 squares, 2½" x 2½"

From the cream tonal fabric, cut:
6 strips, 4½" x 42"
16 strips, 2½" x 42"; crosscut into:
   24 rectangles, 2½" x 12½"
   12 rectangles, 2½" x 8½"
   56 rectangles, 2½" x 4½"
   44 squares, 2½" x 2½"

From the green tonal fabric for vines, cut:
12 bias strips, 1⅛" x 20"

From the orange print, cut:
6 strips, 2¼" x 42"

MAKE THE DARK BLOCKS

The instructions are written for making one dark
block at a time. Repeat the steps to make a total
of four dark blocks.

1. Lightly mark a diagonal line on the wrong side
   of 12 assorted orange or red 2½" squares.
2. Align a marked square with one corner of a
   green floral 4½" square as shown and sew
   along the line. Trim the excess fabric, leaving a
   ¼" seam allowance, and press the seam allowance toward the orange or red triangle. Repeat
   for the remaining three corners of the green
   square to make a center unit.

3. Align a marked orange or red square with one
   end of a tan 2½" x 4½" rectangle as shown
   and sew along the line. Trim the excess fabric
   as before and press the seam allowances
   toward the orange or red triangle. Using a
   second marked square, repeat on the opposite
   end of the tan rectangle to make a flying-geese
   unit. Make four flying-geese units.

Make 4.

4. Arrange the center unit, flying-geese units, and
   four tan polka-dot 2½" squares as shown.
   Sew the pieces in each row together; press
   away from the flying-geese units. Sew the rows
   together to complete a center star unit; press
   away from the center.

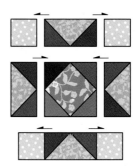 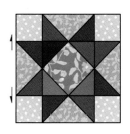

5. Lightly mark a diagonal line on the wrong side
   of four assorted orange or red 2½" squares,
   one from each of four different fabrics. With
   right sides together, align a marked square with
   one tan gingham 2½" square as shown and
   sew along the line. Trim the excess fabric, leaving a ¼" seam allowance, and press toward
   the orange or red triangle. Make four half-
   square-triangle units.

Make 4.

6. Repeat step 3 to make flying-geese units using the green 2½" squares, tan 2½" squares, and brown 2½" x 4½" rectangles. Make four of each as shown.

Make 4.   Make 4.

7. Arrange the two different flying-geese units as shown, placing the tan triangles next to each other. Sew them together to make a side unit. Make four side units.

Make 4.

8. Arrange the center star unit, side units, and half-square-triangle units as shown. Sew the pieces into rows; press toward the side units. Sew the rows together to complete a dark block; press. Make four.

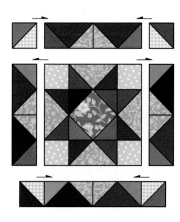

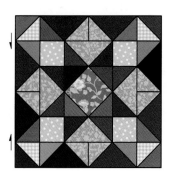

Dark block.
Make 4.

MAKE THE LIGHT BLOCKS

Follow steps 1–8 of "Make the Dark Blocks," referring to the light block assembly diagram below for color and placement. Make a total of five light blocks, using the following fabrics:

⊛ One green floral 4½" square and four assorted brown 2½" squares for the center unit

⊛ Four tan 2½" x 4½" rectangles and eight brown 2½" squares for flying-geese units, and four tan polka-dot 2½" squares for the corners

⊛ Four tan gingham 2½" squares and four assorted orange or red 2½" squares for the half-square-triangle units

⊛ Eight cream tonal 2½" x 4½" rectangles, eight green 2½" squares, and eight tan 2½" squares for the outer flying-geese units

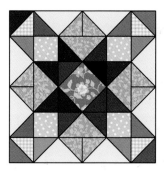

Light block.
Make 5.

ASSEMBLE THE QUILT CENTER

1. Sew two orange or red 1½" x 42" strips together along their long edges to make a strip set; press. Make two. Cut each strip set into 16 segments, 1½" wide, for a total of 32 segments.

1½"

Make 2 strip sets.
Cut 32 segments.

2. Join a segment from each strip set together to make a four-patch unit; press. Make 16 four-patch units.

Make 16.

3. Arrange and sew two light blocks, one dark block, and four cream tonal 2½" x 12½" rectangles, alternating them as shown to make a row. Make two of these rows and press seam allowances toward the cream. Make one row using two dark blocks, one light block, and four cream rectangles. Press toward the cream.

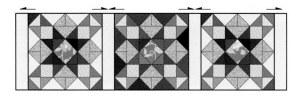

Make 2.

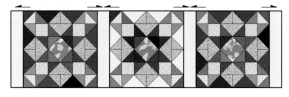

Make 1.

4. Arrange four four-patch units and three cream tonal 2½" x 12½" rectangles as shown. Sew together to make a sashing row; press toward the cream. Make four sashing rows.

Make 4.

5. Referring to the quilt assembly diagram at right, arrange the four sashing rows and three rows of blocks, alternating them as shown. Sew the rows together to complete the quilt center.

ASSEMBLE THE QUILT

1. Lightly mark a diagonal line on the wrong side of 28 assorted orange or red 2½" squares. With right sides together, align a marked square with a cream tonal 2½" square as shown and sew along the line. Trim the excess fabric, leaving a ¼" seam allowance, and press the seam allowance toward the orange or red triangle. Make 28 half-square-triangle units.

Make 28.

2. Arrange six half-square-triangle units, four cream tonal 2½" squares, and three cream tonal 2½" x 8½" rectangles as shown. Sew together to make an inner-border unit; press toward the half-square-triangle units. Make four inner-border units.

Make 4.

3. Sew an inner-border unit to both the left and right edges of the quilt center; press away from the quilt center. Sew a half-square-triangle unit to each end of the remaining two inner-border units as shown; press toward the border unit. Sew these inner-border strips to the top and bottom edges of the quilt center; press away from the quilt center.

4. Sew the cream tonal 4½" x 42" strips together to make one long strip. Cut two strips, 4½" x 48½", and two strips, 4½" x 56½". Sew the 4½" x 48½" border strips to the left and right edges of the quilt; press toward the outer border. Sew the 4½" x 56½" border strips to the top and bottom edges of the quilt; press toward the outer border.

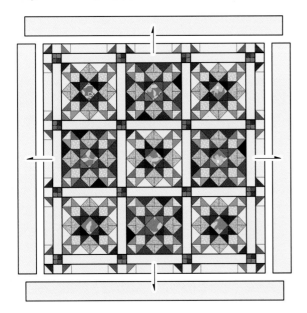

APPLIQUÉ THE BORDER

1. Referring to "Bias Stems and Vines" on page 74, prepare ⅜" bias vines using the green tonal 1⅛"-wide strips.
2. Referring to the appliqué placement diagram below and the pattern on page 58, position three stems and 24 leaves along one side of the quilt. Trim the stems as needed when positioning them. Using the clear monofilament or coordinating thread, stitch the appliqué pieces in place.

Appliqué placement

3. Repeat for each of the remaining three sides of the quilt.

FINISH THE QUILT

For detailed instructions on the following steps, refer to "Finishing Techniques" on page 76.

1. Cut and piece the backing fabric with a horizontal or vertical seam so that it measures 10" larger than both the length and width of the quilt top.
2. Layer the quilt top, batting, and backing together and baste.
3. Machine or hand quilt as desired.
4. Use the orange print 2¼"-wide strips to prepare the binding, and sew the binding to the quilt.

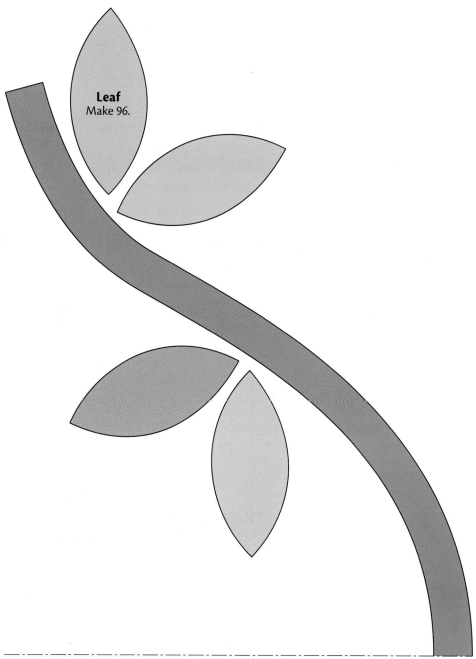

Leaf
Make 96.

Flip pattern along this line.

Designed by Cyndi Walker; pieced by Debbie Gray; quilted by Pamela Dransfeldt

Spring brings picnics, warmer days, and lovely hours spent outside. Piece this fresh, sunny quilt with your scraps, and you'll be doing cartwheels in no time!

FINISHED QUILT: 64½" x 64½"
FINISHED BLOCKS: 16" x 16"

MATERIALS

Yardage is based on 42"-wide fabric.

2⅝ yards of cream tonal fabric for block backgrounds, inner border, and pieced border

¾ yard *total* of assorted aqua prints for four-patch units and pieced border

⅝ yard of pink floral for Pinwheel blocks and Star blocks

⅝ yard of tan dot fabric for Pinwheel blocks and Star blocks

½ yard of tan floral for Pinwheel blocks and pieced border

½ yard *total* of assorted cream prints for four-patch units

½ yard of dark-pink fabric for Star blocks

1 fat quarter* of pink fabric for pieced border

⅝ yard of cream striped fabric for binding

4⅛ yards of fabric for backing

74" x 74" piece of batting

A 10" x 10" square from your stash is also sufficient.

CUT THE FABRICS

From the cream tonal fabric, cut:
11 strips, 4½" x 42"; cut 5 of the strips into 20 rectangles, 4½" x 8½"
4 squares, 9¼" x 9¼", cut each square into quarters diagonally to make 16 triangles
4 strips, 4⅞" x 42"; crosscut into 28 squares, 4⅞" x 4⅞". Cut each square in half diagonally to make 56 triangles.
5 squares, 5¼" x 5¼"; cut each square into quarters diagonally to make 20 triangles

From the pink floral, cut:
5 squares, 9¼" x 9¼"; cut each square into quarters diagonally to make 20 triangles
5 squares, 4½" x 4½"

From the tan floral, cut:
1 strip, 4⅞" x 42"; crosscut into 8 squares, 4⅞" x 4⅞". Cut each square in half diagonally to make 16 triangles.
1 square, 9¼" x 9¼"; cut into quarters diagonally to make 4 triangles
2 squares, 4½" x 4½"

From the tan dot fabric, cut:

1 strip, 4⅞" x 42"; crosscut into 8 squares, 4⅞" x 4⅞". Cut each square in half diagonally to make 16 triangles.

2 strips, 2½" x 42"; crosscut into 20 squares, 2½" x 2½"

1 square, 9¼" x 9¼"; cut into quarters diagonally to make 4 triangles

2 squares, 4½" x 4½"

From the assorted aqua prints, cut:

72 squares, 2½" x 2½"

2 squares, 9¼" x 9¼"; cut each square into quarters diagonally to make 8 triangles

From the assorted cream prints, cut:

72 squares, 2½" x 2½"

From the pink fat quarter, cut:

1 square, 9¼" x 9¼"; cut into quarters diagonally to make 4 triangles

From the dark-pink fabric, cut:

2 strips, 2⅞" x 42"; crosscut into 20 squares, 2⅞" x 2⅞". Cut each square in half diagonally to make 40 triangles.

1 square, 9¼" x 9¼"; cut into quarters diagonally to make 4 triangles

From the cream striped fabric, cut:

7 strips, 2¼" x 42"

MAKE THE FOUR-PATCH UNITS

Arrange two assorted aqua and two assorted cream 2½" squares together as shown and sew together into rows; press toward the aqua. Sew the rows together to make a four-patch unit. Make 36 four-patch units.

Make 36.

MAKE THE PINWHEEL BLOCKS

1. Arrange one tan floral 4⅞" triangle, one tan dot 4⅞" triangle, and one four-patch unit as shown. Sew the tan dot triangle to the four-patch unit; press toward the triangle. Sew the tan floral triangle to the adjacent edge of the four-patch unit and press. Make 16.

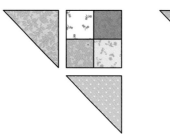 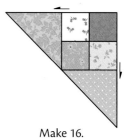

Make 16.

2. Arrange one pink floral and one cream 9¼" triangle as shown and sew together along the short edges; press toward the pink. Make 16.

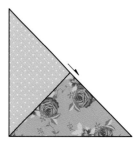

Make 16.

3. Sew the unit from step 2 to the unit from step 1; press away from the four-patch triangle unit. Make 16.

 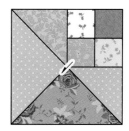

Make 16.

4. Arrange four of the units from step 3 as shown. Sew the units into rows; press seam allowances in each row in opposite directions. Sew the rows together to make a Pinwheel block; press. Make four Pinwheel blocks.

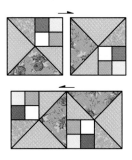
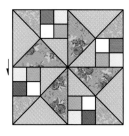

Make 4.

MAKE THE STAR BLOCKS

1. Sew a dark-pink 2⅞" triangle to one diagonal edge of a cream 5¼" triangle; press toward the pink. Sew a dark-pink triangle to the opposite diagonal edge of the cream triangle to make a flying-geese unit; press toward the pink. Make 20 flying-geese units.

Make 20.

2. Arrange four tan dot squares, four flying-geese units, and one pink floral 4½" square as shown. Sew the pieces in each row together; press away from the flying-geese units. Sew the rows together to make a star unit. Make five star units.

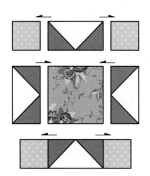

Make 5.

3. Arrange four four-patch units, four cream 4½" x 8½" rectangles, and one star unit as shown. Sew the units in each row together; press toward the cream rectangles. Sew the rows together to make a Star block. Make five Star blocks.

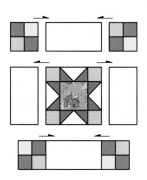
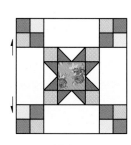

Make 5.

MAKE THE PIECED BORDERS

1. Using two cream 4⅞" triangles and one pink, aqua, or tan 9¼" triangle, make a flying-geese unit as you did for the Star blocks. Make 28 flying-geese units for the borders.

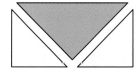
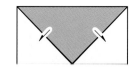

Make 28.

2. Sew seven flying-geese units together as shown to make a pieced border; press seam allowances in one direction. Make four.

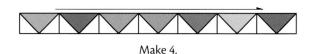

Make 4.

ASSEMBLE THE QUILT

1. Referring to the quilt assembly diagram on the opposite page, sew together the four Pinwheel blocks and five Star blocks into three rows of three blocks each; press toward the Star blocks. Sew the rows together to complete the quilt center; press in one direction.

2. Sew the cream tonal 4½" x 42" strips together to make one long strip. Cut two strips, 4½" x 48½", and two strips, 4½" x 56½". Sew the 4½" x 48½" strips to the left and right sides of the quilt; press toward the border. Sew the 4½" x 56½" strips to the top and bottom of the quilt; press toward the border.

3. Sew a pieced border strip to both the left and right sides of the quilt; press toward the inner border. Using the tan floral and tan dot 4½" squares, sew a square to each end of the two remaining pieced border strips; press toward the square. Sew these strips to the top and bottom of the quilt; press toward the inner border.

FINISH THE QUILT

For detailed instructions on the following steps, refer to "Finishing Techniques" on page 76.

1. Cut and piece the backing fabric with a vertical or horizontal seam so that it measures 10" larger than both the length and width of the quilt top.

2. Layer the quilt top, batting, and backing together and baste.

3. Machine or hand quilt as desired.

4. Use the cream striped 2¼"-wide strips to prepare the binding, and sew the binding to the quilt.

Moonflowers

Designed and appliquéd by Cyndi Walker; pieced by Debbie Gray; quilted by Kate Sullivan

*E*voking the beguiling blooms that appear by night, this quilt features a print with a dark background to let the flowers really shine. Cream stars twinkle against the elegant floral print and the blooms unfurl around the border. Make the most of one of your favorite large-scale floral prints and give this quilt a try!

MATERIALS

Yardage is based on 42"-wide fabric.

1 ⅞ yards of red floral for Star blocks and Flower blocks
1 ½ yards of cream tonal fabric for Star blocks
½ yard of blue floral for Star blocks
½ yard of tan dot fabric for Star blocks
⅜ yard of tan floral for inner border
⅜ yard of light-blue tonal fabric for inner border
⅓ yard of blue tonal fabric for Flower blocks
¼ yard *each* of 2 tan prints for four-patch units
¼ yard *each* of 2 cream prints for four-patch units
¼ yard of cream floral for Flower block centers
1 fat quarter of green tonal fabric for appliquéd stems
⅛ yard or scraps of green dot fabric for appliquéd leaves
⅛ yard or scraps of red solid for appliquéd flower centers
⅝ yard of blue print for binding
4⅛ yards of fabric for backing
74" x 74" piece of batting
½" bias bar
Clear monofilament or matching embroidery thread for machine appliqué
Water-soluble glue

CUT THE FABRICS

Patterns for the flower center and leaf are on page 70.

From the red floral, cut:

11 squares, 9¼" x 9¼"; cut each square into quarters diagonally to make 44 triangles
4 squares, 5¼" x 5¼"; cut each square into quarters diagonally to make 16 triangles
3 strips, 4½" x 42"; cut into:
    8 rectangles, 4½" x 8½"
    8 squares, 4½" x 4½"
4 strips, 2½" x 42"; cut into:
    8 rectangles, 2½" x 6½"
    8 rectangles, 2½" x 4½"
    24 squares, 2½" x 2½"

Continued on page 66.

From the cream tonal fabric, cut:
2 strips, 5¼" x 42"; crosscut into 12 squares, 5¼" x 5¼". Cut each square into quarters diagonally to make 48 triangles.
6 strips, 4⅞" x 42"; crosscut into 44 squares, 4⅞" x 4⅞". Cut each square in half diagonally to make 88 triangles.
3 strips, 2½" x 42"; crosscut into 48 squares, 2½" x 2½"

From the blue floral, cut:
4 strips, 2⅞" x 42"; crosscut into 48 squares, 2⅞" x 2⅞". Cut each square in half diagonally to make 96 triangles.

From the tan dot fabric, cut:
4 strips, 2⅞" x 42"; crosscut into 48 squares, 2⅞" x 2⅞". Cut each square in half diagonally to make 96 triangles.

From *each* of the 2 tan prints, cut:
2 strips, 2½" x 42" (4 total)

From *each* of the 2 cream prints, cut:
2 strips, 2½" x 42" (4 total)

From the blue tonal fabric, cut:
2 strips, 2⅞" x 42"; crosscut into 16 squares, 2⅞" x 2⅞". Cut each square in half diagonally to make 32 triangles.
1 strip, 2½" x 42"; crosscut into 16 squares, 2½" x 2½"

From the cream floral, cut:
1 strip, 4½" x 42"; crosscut into 8 squares, 4½" x 4½"

From the green tonal fabric, cut:
8 bias strips, 1⅜" x 18"

From the green dot fabric, cut:
16 leaves

From the red solid, cut:
8 flower centers

From the light-blue tonal fabric, cut:
4 strips, 2½" x 32½"

From the tan floral, cut:
4 strips, 2½" x 32½"

From the blue print for binding, cut:
7 strips, 2¼" x 42"

MAKE THE STAR BLOCKS

1. Sew a blue floral triangle and a tan dot triangle together along their long edges to make a half-square-triangle unit; press seam allowances toward the blue fabric. Make 48 half-square-triangle units.

Make 48.

2. Arrange four half-square-triangle units into a pinwheel as shown. Sew the units in each row together; press the seam allowances in opposite directions. Sew the rows together and press. Make 12 pinwheel units.

Make 12.

3. Sew a tan dot triangle to the short edge of a cream tonal 5¼" triangle as shown; press toward the tan. Sew a blue floral triangle to the other diagonal edge to make a flying-geese unit; press toward the blue. Make 48 cream, tan, and blue flying-geese units.

Make 48.

4. Arrange four cream tonal 2½" squares, four blue-and-tan flying-geese units, and one pinwheel unit as shown. Sew the pieces in each row together; press toward the flying-geese units. Sew the rows together to make a center star unit; press. Make 12 center star units.

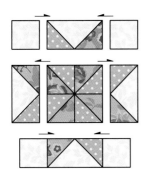
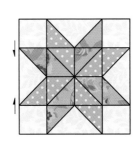

Make 12.

5. With right sides together, sew a tan print strip and a cream print strip together along their long edges; press toward the tan to make a strip set. Make two identical strip sets. Repeat with the remaining tan and cream strips to make a total of four cream-and-tan strip sets. Cut each strip set into 16 segments, 2½" wide, to make a total of 64 segments.

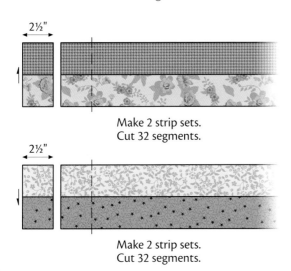

2½"

Make 2 strip sets.
Cut 32 segments.

2½"

Make 2 strip sets.
Cut 32 segments.

6. Arrange one segment from each of the different strip sets as shown and sew together to make a four-patch unit; press. Make 32 four-patch units.

Make 32.

7. Sew a cream tonal 4⅞" triangle to one short edge of a red floral 9¼" triangle; press toward the red. Sew a second cream tonal triangle to the other short edge to make a flying-geese unit; press toward the red. Repeat to make 44 red-and-cream flying-geese units.

Make 44.

8. Arrange four red-and-cream flying-geese units, four four-patch units, and one center star unit as shown. Sew the units in each row together; press toward the flying-geese units. Sew the rows together to make a Star block; press away from the center star unit. Make eight Star blocks.

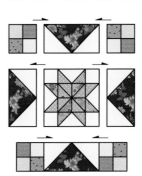

Make 8.

9. To make the partial Star blocks for the sides, arrange two red floral 4½" squares, three red-and-cream flying-geese units, and one center star unit as shown. Sew the units in each row together; press toward the flying-geese units. Sew the rows together to make a block; press away from the center star unit. Make four partial Star blocks for the sides.

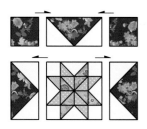

Make 4.

MAKE THE FLOWER BLOCKS

1. Sew a blue tonal triangle to one diagonal edge of a small red floral triangle; press toward the blue. Sew a second blue tonal triangle to the other diagonal edge of the red floral triangle to make a blue-and-red flying-geese unit; press toward the blue. Make 16 blue-and-red flying-geese units.

Make 16.

2. Lightly mark a diagonal line on the wrong side of each blue tonal 2½" square.

3. Align a marked square with one end of a red floral 2½" x 4½" rectangle as shown and sew along the line. Trim the excess fabric, leaving a ¼" seam allowance, and press toward the blue to make a short flower unit. Make four left and four right short flower units.

Make 4 of each.

4. Repeat step 3 using a blue tonal 2½" square and a red floral 2½" x 6½" rectangle to make a long flower unit. Make four left and four right long flower units.

Make 4 of each.

5. Arrange three red floral 2½" squares, two blue-and-red flying-geese units, one cream floral 4½" square, one left short flower unit, one left long flower unit, and a red floral 4½" x 8½" rectangle as shown. Sew the units in each row together; press toward the squares. Sew the rows together to make a flower unit; press away from the cream square. Make four left flower blocks.

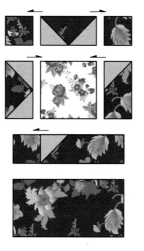 

Left flower block.
Make 4.

6. Repeat step 5 using the right short and long flower units to make four right flower blocks.

Right flower block.
Make 4.

APPLIQUÉ THE FLOWER BLOCKS

1. Referring to "Bias Stems and Vines" on page 74, prepare ½" bias stems using the green tonal 1⅜"-wide bias strips.

2. Referring to the appliqué placement diagrams below, position a stem, two leaves, and one flower center in each flower block. Trim the stems as needed. Using clear monofilament or coordinating thread, stitch the appliqué pieces in place. Repeat for each of the eight flower blocks.

Left flower block   Right flower block
Appliqué placement

ASSEMBLE THE QUILT

1. Arrange one left flower block, one right flower block, one partial Star block, one light-blue 2½" x 32½" strip, and one tan floral 2½" x 32½" strip as shown above right.

2. Sew the flower blocks and partial Star block together; press toward the flower blocks. Sew the blue and tan strips to the bottom of the blocks; press toward the strips to make a side unit. Make four side units.

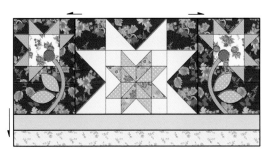

Make 4.

3. Arrange four Star blocks into two rows of two blocks each. Sew the blocks in each row together; press in opposite directions. Sew the rows together to make the quilt center.

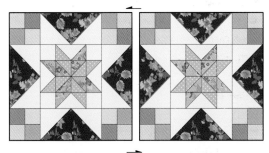

4. Sew a side unit to both the left and right edges of the quilt center; press toward the side units.

5. Sew a Star block to each end of the remaining side units; press toward the side unit. Sew these units to the top and bottom of the quilt center; press away from the quilt center.

FINISH THE QUILT

For detailed instructions on the following steps, refer to "Finishing Techniques" on page 76.

1. Cut and piece the backing fabric with a horizontal or vertical seam so that it measures 10" larger than both the length and width of the quilt top.

2. Layer the quilt top, batting, and backing together and baste.

3. Machine or hand quilt as desired.

4. Use the blue print 2¼"-wide strips to prepare the binding, and sew the binding to the quilt.

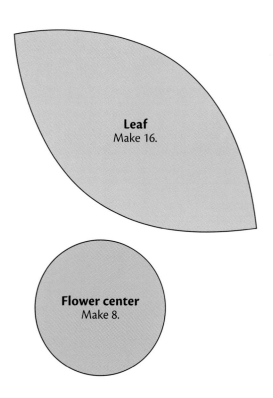

Leaf
Make 16.

Flower center
Make 8.

Quiltmaking Basics

This section includes information about the basic tools and techniques you'll rely on to make the quilts in this book. Read through it before beginning a project and refer back to it as needed while you're working on your quilt.

SUPPLIES

Stock your sewing room with the following basic supplies and you'll be ready to jump right in any time you have a few minutes to sit down and stitch.

Sewing machine. A sewing machine in good working order, with a reliable, even straight stitch, is key to any quilting project. A few "bells and whistles," such as a blanket or zigzag stitch for machine appliqué and the ability to lower your feed dogs for free-motion quilting, are nice features for quilting.

Acrylic rulers. Generally, the size ruler you'll need will depend on the size of your project. For the projects in this book, a 6½" x 12" ruler is very handy for general cutting, while an 8½" x 24" ruler is perfect for cutting borders and squaring up your quilt. As you continue to make quilts, you may find other sizes helpful for making your tasks go more smoothly. Whatever size ruler you choose, be sure the grid lines are clearly visible when you place the ruler on your fabric.

Rotary cutter and mat. A rotary cutter with a sharp blade and a mat designed for cutting are must-haves for today's quilter. The cutting mat should be big enough to accommodate larger pieces of fabric comfortably. If you encounter issues with your blade not cutting through all layers of your fabric, replace the blade—it's probably nicked or dull.

Pins and needles. Sharp, extra-fine silk pins with glass heads are the best choice for holding fabric pieces in place as you sew. Because they're sharp and thin, they glide through the fabric and reduce the shifting of matched points.

As for needles, keep a variety—including basting needles—on hand for all types of sewing. For hand appliqué, a 10 or 11 Sharp works well. For general machine piecing, an 80/12 Sharp needle is a good choice.

Thread. Cotton thread in a neutral color is a good choice for piecing. If you're working with dark fabric, you may want to consider a darker thread to avoid any stitches showing through when the seams are pressed.

For machine appliqué and quilting, you can use a wide range of thread fibers and colors depending on the look you wish to achieve. Rayon thread provides a nice sheen, while cotton thread has a clean, crisp finish. Experiment with both on a test piece of fabric to determine which you would like to use for each project.

For hand appliqué, 50-weight or 60-weight cotton thread works well. Coordinate the color with your appliqué piece rather than with the background fabric.

Scissors. A sharp pair of scissors is a must for cutting fabric and appliqué pieces. Consider keeping a smaller pair of embroidery scissors on hand as well for snipping threads and cutting curves. Using sewing scissors to cut paper dulls them quickly, so it's a good idea to reserve one pair of scissors just for paper.

Seam ripper. As much as we hate to admit it, we all need a seam ripper from time to time to assist in removing stitches from pieces sewn together incorrectly.

Marking tools. For marking quilting designs on a finished quilt top, I find that chalk works best. Water-soluble markers or quilter's pencils are also helpful tools for marking fabric. A mechanical pencil with a soft lead comes in handy for tracing templates onto fabric. Whatever markers you plan to use, test them first on a scrap of fabric to be sure they're easy to see and—if necessary—easy to remove.

ROTARY CUTTING

Quilting has changed enormously with the advent of the rotary cutter, which allows you to quickly and precisely cut fabric into strips, rectangles, squares, and triangles.

Press your fabric and fold it in half, selvage to selvage. (If you're working with a large piece of fabric, you may wish to fold the fabric in half once again by bringing the folded edge to meet the selvage.)

Place the folded edges of the fabric along a horizontal line on your cutting mat. Place a small square ruler along the folded edge of your fabric and place your long ruler over the left edge of the fabric, aligning the right edge of the ruler with the square ruler and a vertical line on the cutting mat. Remove the square ruler and use your rotary cutter to trim and straighten the edge of the fabric, making sure that you're cutting through all layers.

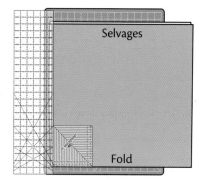

Many projects in this book instruct you to cut a strip of fabric and then crosscut it into squares and rectangles. To do this, cut the strip as indicated in the instructions, and then align the long cut edge of the strip with a horizontal line on your cutting mat. Use your ruler and rotary cutter to trim the short edge of the strip. Measure the correct size, and cut the strip into smaller segments.

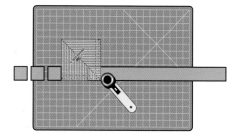

To cut half-square triangles from squares, align your ruler diagonally over the square from corner to corner and cut the square in half to create two triangles. If the directions call for quarter-square triangles, carefully align the ruler diagonally in the opposite direction and make a second cut.

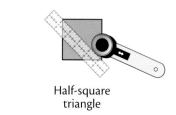

Half-square triangle

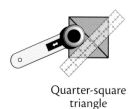

Quarter-square triangle

MACHINE PIECING

The success of any quilting project relies on a precise and consistent ¼" seam. If your sewing machine has a ¼"-wide foot, you'll find it easier to maintain accuracy. If your machine is not equipped with this attachment, you may be able to set the position of the needle to accommodate this width. You may also create a ¼" seam guide by measuring and then placing a piece of tape ¼" to the right of the needle as shown.

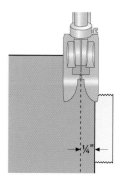

If you find that your finished units and blocks are not aligning correctly or are not quite measuring up, it may be that the ¼" seam is slightly off. Seam variances, even as little as ¹⁄₁₆", will multiply as you go along. This is especially true for smaller pieces and more complicated blocks. If you're unsure about the setting on your machine, try sewing along the edge of a scrap of fabric and then measuring the distance between the stitch line and the raw edge of the fabric. Adjust as necessary to achieve the perfect ¼" seam.

Chain Piecing

When you need to make large numbers of identical units, chain piecing can provide an efficient means of reaching your goal. Chain piecing is based on the assembly-line principle. Instead of stopping and clipping the thread between each unit, continue to stitch identical pieces in a chain-linked fashion, stopping to cut them apart only when you've reached the correct number of like units. This allows you to continue sewing without interruption.

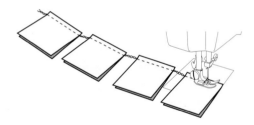

Strip Piecing

You can make quick work of certain patchwork units and blocks by utilizing strip sets. This technique consists of sewing two or more strips of fabric together along their long edges and then crosscutting the strip sets into units or segments.

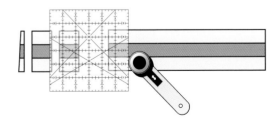

Smart Sewing

If you're sewing more than two strips together at one time, try sewing from opposite ends of the strip each time you join a new strip to avoid "warping" in your strip set. (Arrows indicate stitching directions).

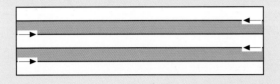

Working with Triangles

Triangles have a reputation among quilters as being difficult to work with due to the stretch-prone bias edge created when the fabric is cut on a 45° angle. Once mastered, however, triangles can open doors to new and exciting quilts.

To minimize distortion, handle triangles with care as you piece and press them. Many stray triangle points are caused by a last-minute flip in the direction of the seam allowance when the seam is sewn. To avoid this, use the tip of your seam ripper to hold the seam allowance in place as you sew. With a little practice, you'll be on your way to perfect points and accurate seam intersections.

Pinning Pointer

Pinning triangles together can help you keep your points in check. Try to avoid the temptation to sew without pinning, especially on small triangles.

Pressing

Mastering the art of pressing can make all the difference in achieving accuracy in patchwork. The key is to remember that pressing is not the same as ironing. Resist the urge to drag the iron back and forth; instead, lift and set it down while applying downward pressure. This method can help prevent distortion of the fabric, especially when you're working with the bias edges of triangles. The addition of steam during this process is also helpful for ensuring a crisply pressed block.

The general rule of thumb is to press seams toward the darkest fabric to avoid any dark colors showing through the lighter fabrics. Instructions and diagrams for each project include pressing guidelines to assist you.

MACHINE APPLIQUÉ

Some of the quilts in this book feature appliqué. I use a great machine technique that gives the look of hand or needle-turn appliqué. This method involves using freezer paper for your templates. In addition to freezer paper, the supplies needed are minimal—a little liquid fabric starch, a small brush or cotton swab for applying the starch, and an iron. A small travel iron, if you have one, works great for this.

1. Trace your appliqué template with pencil, in reverse, onto the paper side of the freezer paper. Cut the pieces out along the line.
2. Using a dry iron, press the piece onto the wrong side of the fabric you've chosen for your appliqué. Cut out the shape adding a scant ¼" seam allowance around the edge of the template.

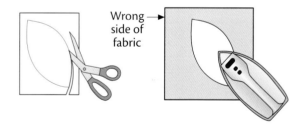

3. Using your brush or cotton swab, apply the fabric starch along the outside edge of the fabric, making sure the starch does not reach the paper template. The fabric will soak up the starch.

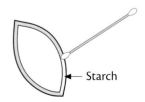

← Starch

Less Is Best

To avoid distorted appliqué shapes, try to keep your freezer paper dry and free of starch. Use a light touch with the starch for best results.

4. Fold the fabric over the edge of the paper template and gently iron into place, folding the fabric as you go along. Let the piece cool, and remove the freezer-paper template. Gently position the folded fabric back into place. Now you're ready to appliqué!

5. Position the prepared appliqué piece onto your background fabric and use water-soluble appliqué glue to hold it in place. Repeat with all the appliqué pieces for your project.
6. With coordinating thread or invisible thread, and a very small blanket stitch, sew along the outside of each piece to secure all of the edges. You can also use a narrow zigzag stitch.

BIAS STEMS AND VINES

Bias stems and vines are remarkably easy to make, and their slightly three-dimensional look can add a lot of character to your appliqué project. They can be appliquéd by hand or machine. My preferred method for making bias stems is with a special set of metal pressing bars. I've seen several types, made by different manufacturers, but I personally prefer the metal bars from Celtic Design. You can buy them in sets of varying widths. Special notions like this are always a personal choice, so if you already own a set of bias bars and they work well for you, by all means feel free to use them.

To make bias vines or stems, first calculate the width of bias strips to cut. Don't worry—it's easy! Just take the desired finished width of the bias strip, double that number, and add ⅜" to it. For instance, if you want a ½"-wide finished bias vine, it would be: ½" x 2 = 1"; 1" + ⅜" = 1⅜". So you'd need to cut a 1⅜"-wide strip on the bias (at a 45° angle to the straight grain). For the quilts in this book, just follow the cutting instructions provided with each project. If you'd like to make different widths or include them in your appliqué designs for other projects, you'll know how!

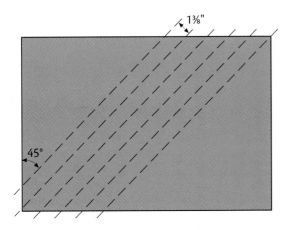

Once you've cut your strip on the bias, gently fold the strip in half, wrong sides together so that the raw edges align. Sew a ⅛" seam along the raw edges the entire length of the strip. Insert your bias bar of the appropriate width (½" for this example) and press firmly, centering the seam allowance on one side, to create a crisp edge. You're all done!

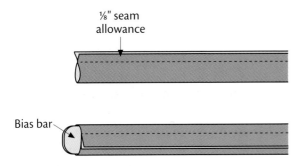

BORDERS

When you've finished assembling the center area of your quilt, it's time to add the borders (if the project includes them). The instructions for each project give you the appropriate cutting instructions for single-fabric borders. However, since your cutting and piecing may have created slight variations in the project dimensions, it's always a good idea to measure your quilt before you cut the borders to ensure the best possible fit. This involves taking a measurement in three places: along the right (or top) edge, through the center, and along the left (or bottom) edge. I take three measurements because the edges of the quilt may have stretched slightly during handling.

1. Measure the length of the quilt top through the center and along the two parallel outside edges. If the three measurements do not match, figure the average, and then cut the side border strips to this measurement. Find and mark the midpoints of the border strips and the side edges of the quilt. Place the border strips right sides together with the sides of the quilt, matching the ends and midpoints, and pin in place. Sew and press as instructed, usually toward the border strips.

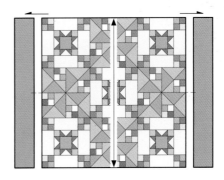

2. Measure the width of the quilt top through the center, including the side borders you just added; measure the two parallel outside edges as well. Average the measurements if necessary, and then cut the top and bottom border strips to this measurement. Find and mark the midpoints of the border strips and the top and bottom edges of the quilt. Place the border strips right sides together with the top

and bottom of the quilt, matching the ends and midpoints; pin, sew, and press.

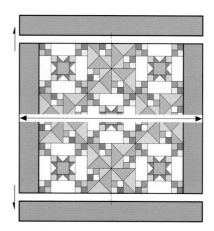

FINISHING TECHNIQUES

You've put so much care into choosing the fabrics and assembling your quilt top, you'll want to make sure your quilting and binding techniques don't let you down. Here are some techniques to help you achieve a perfect finish.

Assembling the Layers

Cut the quilt backing to measure 10" larger than the quilt in both length and width to allow for any shrinking that might occur during the quilting process. The materials list for each project includes the appropriate amount of fabric to purchase for the backing. For all of the quilts in this book, you'll need to piece the backing.

1. Cut the fabric crosswise into two pieces of equal length. Remove the selvages and sew the pieces together using a ½" seam. Press the seam allowances open.

2. Spread the backing, wrong side up, on a clean, flat surface. Secure the edges of the backing to the work surface with masking tape to keep the backing fabric smooth.

3. Center the batting and quilt top, right side up, over the backing, smoothing each layer as you go to avoid any puckering during the quilting process.

4. Working from the center of the quilt out toward the edges, baste the layers together. For machine quilting, use safety pins to hold the

three layers together, spacing the pins approximately 6" apart. For hand quilting, use a light-colored thread and large basting stitches to secure the layers.

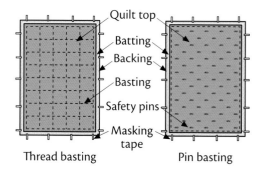

Thread basting   Pin basting

Machine Quilting

The quilts in this book were quilted by machine, which is a great way to finish your projects quickly. For quilting straight lines, a walking foot helps to prevent puckering or shifting of the fabric layers as you quilt. I suggest that you test your machine's tension, needle, thread, and stitch quality by quilting on a small sandwich of batting and fabric from your current project before stitching on your quilt.

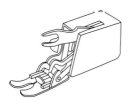

Walking foot

Some common straight-stitch designs include stitching in the ditch (stitching right along the seam line in key seams and around each shape) and outline quilting (stitching ¼" from the seam lines in each shape). These techniques are often used to highlight traditional designs or special piecing.

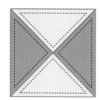

Quilting in the ditch   Outline quilting

For free-motion quilting, you need a machine with a darning foot and the capability to lower the feed dogs. With this technique, you guide the quilt in the direction of the design, rather than relying on the feed dogs to move the quilt.

Darning foot

An easy way to get started with free-motion quilting is with a stipple or meander pattern. For quilts with appliqué, try stitching around the edges of the pieces to outline or highlight the shapes.

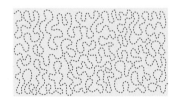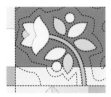

Free-motion quilting

Stitching Success

When free-motion quilting, use a single-hole throat plate on your machine, if you have one, rather than a zigzag throat plate. This will give you better stitch quality.

For further guidance on machine-quilting techniques, an excellent resource is *Machine Quilting Made Easy!* by Maurine Noble (Martingale & Company, 1994).

Binding

For all of the projects in this book, I used the traditional French-fold method of binding. Each project lists adequate yardage for 2¼"-wide crosswise strips to cover the perimeter of the quilt, plus an additional 10" for seams, folding at the corners, and overlapping. This will give you a binding that finishes at about ⅜" wide. If you want a wider binding, cut wider strips.

1. Cut the binding fabric across its width into 2¼"-wide strips as directed in the cutting list for your project.

2. Piece the binding strips together end to end at right angles as shown to make a continuous strip. Trim any excess seam allowance to ¼" and press the seams open to reduce bulk. When you've sewn all the strips together, fold the strip in half lengthwise, wrong sides together, and press. Trim one end at a 45° angle, fold the trimmed end under, and press along the fold.

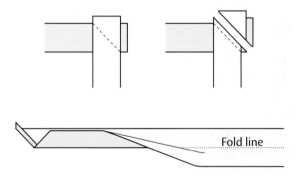

Fold line

3. Trim the batting and backing even with the quilt top. Place the binding on one side of the quilt top, with right sides together and raw edges aligned. Begin a few inches from the start of the binding strip (this end will be used later to create a smooth end to the binding), and stitch the binding to the quilt using a ¼"-wide seam allowance.

4. Stop stitching ¼" from the first corner, backstitch, raise the needle, and clip the thread. Rotate the quilt 90°. Fold the binding up, away from the quilt, and then back down onto itself, parallel with the edge of the quilt top. Resume sewing with a backstitch at the edge of the

quilt. This creates a miter in the binding when you finish the corners in step 6.

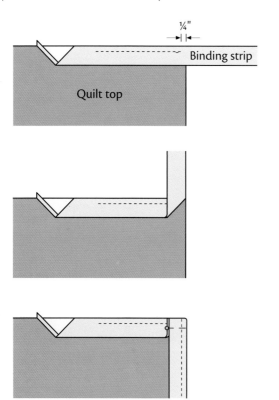

Pin for Perfection

When you rotate the binding at the corner to miter it, try pinning the fold in place to keep it secure and ensure a crisper corner.

5. Continue sewing the binding to the edges of the quilt, repeating steps 3 and 4 at each corner. Stop sewing when you're approximately 1" from the starting point of the binding. Overlap the starting point by 1" to 2", trim the excess binding at a 45° angle, and tuck the tail into the folded diagonal edge. Finish the binding seam.

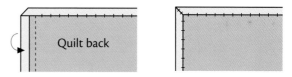

6. Fold the binding over the raw edges to the back of the quilt so that the edge of the binding covers the machine stitching. Use matching thread to blindstitch the folded edge of the binding in place and blindstitch the mitered corners.

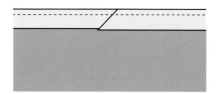

About the Author

Cyndi Walker was born in California and received a degree in fashion art from Virginia Commonwealth University. Always active in the creative arts, she was working as a graphic designer and illustrator when she found a unique outlet for her talents in quilting. From her very first quilting class she was hooked, and ever since she has enjoyed seeking out new and exciting fabrics as well as inspiration for her own patterns and fabric designs. Cyndi owns a quilt-pattern company, Stitch Studios, and designs fabric for Riley Blake Designs. She lives in the Seattle area with her family and two dogs.

Cyndi Walker of Stitch Studios

There's More Online!

Visit Cyndi's website at www.stitchstudios.com. Find more books on quilting at www.martingale-pub.com.